Nelson Literacy

Senior Author
Jennette MacKenzie

Senior Consultant
Miriam P. Trehearne

Senior Consultant
Carmel Crévola

Series Consultants
Ruth McQuirter Scott—*Word Study*
James Coulter—*Assessment*
Neil Andersen—*Media*
Maureen Innes—*ESL/ELL*
Rod Peturson—*Science*
Nancy Christoffer—*Bias and Equity*

Series Writing Team
Paula S. Goepfert, *Senior Writer*
Marg Camp
Kathleen Corrigan
James Coulter
Dianne Dillabough
Lalie Harcourt
Jane Hutchison
Karen Kahler
Norma Kennedy
Christel Kleitsch
Wendy Mathieu
Christine McClymont
Heather McGowan
Bev McMorris
Thérèse McNamara
Sarah Peterson
Liz Powell
Mary Schoones
Ricki Wortzman

NELSON EDUCATION

NELSON EDUCATION

Nelson Literacy 6a
Jennette MacKenzie

Associate Vice President, Publishing and Customer Solutions
Beverley Buxton

General Manager, Literacy and Reference
Kevin Martindale

Director of Publishing, Literacy and Reference
Joe Banel

Publisher, Literacy
Rivka Cranley

Executive Managing Editor, Development
Darleen Rotozinski

Senior Product Manager
Mark Cressman

Program Managers
Barbara Hehner
Tracey MacDonald

Project Editor
Lara Caplan

Developmental Editors
Laura Edlund
David MacDonald

Researchers
Susan Hughes
Catherine Rondina

Assistant Editors
Petal Almeida
Corry Codner

Editorial Assistants
Adam Rennie
Kristen Sanchioni

Executive Director, Content and Media Production
Renate McCloy

Director, Content and Media Production
Lisa Dimson

Senior Content Production Manager
Carol Martin

Content Production Editor
Christi Davis-Martell

Proofreader
Elizabeth D'Anjou

Production Manager
Cathy Deak

Director, Asset Management Services
Vicki Gould

Design Director
Ken Phipps

Managing Designer
Sasha Moroz

Series Design
Sasha Moroz
Steven Savicky

Series Wordmark
Steven Savicky

Cover Design
Sasha Moroz

Interior Design
Jarrel Breckon
Brian Cartwright
Claudia Davila
Courtney Hellam
Karin Hincks
Jennifer Laing
Eugene Lo
Sasha Moroz
Roberto Pagliero
Peter Papayanakis
Peggy Rhodes
Jan John Rivera
Studio Montage
Glenn Toddun

Art Buyer
Suzanne Peden

Compositor
Courtney Hellam

Photo Research and Permissions
Lisa Brant

Printer
Transcontinental Printing

ISBN-13: 978-0-17-629118-1
ISBN-10: 0-17-629118-0

Printed and bound in Canada
2 3 4 11 10 09 08

For more information contact Nelson Education Ltd., 1120 Birchmount Road, Toronto, Ontario, M1K 5G4. Or you can visit our Internet site at http://www.nelson.com

Advisers and Reviewers: Ontario

Nora Alexander

Stephanie Aubertin, Limestone DSB

Gale Bankowski, Hamilton-Wentworth CDSB

Wendy Bedford, Peterborough Victoria Northumberland and Clarington CDSB

Trudy Bell, Grand Erie DSB

Debra Boddy, Toronto DSB

Maggie Boss, Dufferin-Peel CDSB

Michelle Bryden, Eastern Ontario CDSB

Elizabeth M. Burchat, Renfrew CDSB

Karen Byromshaw, Toronto DSB

Mary Cairo, Toronto CDSB

Cheryl Chapman, Avon Maitland DSB

Cathy Chaput, Wellington CDSB

Christina Clancy, Dufferin-Peel CDSB

Alison Cooke, Grand Erie DSB

Cheryl Cristobal, Dufferin-Peel CDSB

Genevieve Dowson, Hamilton-Wentworth CDSB

Denise Edwards, Toronto DSB

Lorraine Giroux, District School Board of Niagara

Charmaine Graves, Thames Valley DSB

Colleen Hayward, Toronto CDSB

Charmaine Hung, Toronto DSB

Eddie Ing, Toronto DSB

Sue Jackson, Thames Valley DSB

Lee Jones-Imhotep, Toronto DSB

Ray King, Dufferin-Peel CDSB

Tanya Korostil, Peel DSB

Rocky Landon, Limestone DSB

Helen Lavigne, Waterloo CDSB

Luci Lackey, Upper Grand DSB

Laurie Light, Dufferin-Peel CDSB

Lorrie Lowes, Ottawa-Carleton DSB

Maria Makuch, Ottawa-Carleton DSB

Jennifer Mandarino, Dufferin-Peel CDSB

Carolyn March, Hamilton-Wentworth DSB

Mary Marshall, Halton DSB

Claire McDowell, Lambton Kent DSB

Thérèse McNamara, Simcoe County DSB

Andrew Mildenberger, Toronto DSB

Laura Mossey, Durham DSB

Elisena Mycroft, Hamilton-Wentworth DSB

Mary Anne Olah, Toronto DSB

Judy Onody, Toronto CDSB

Eleanor Pardoe, Grand Erie DSB

Krista Pedersen, Upper Canada DSB

Sarah Peterson, Waterloo DSB

Annemarie Petrasek, Huron Perth CDSB

Catherine Pollock, Toronto DSB

Cheryl Potvin, Ottawa-Carleton DSB

Amarjit Rai, Peel DSB

Tara Rajaram-Donaldson, Toronto DSB

Kelly Rilley, Windsor-Essex CDSB

Joanne Saragosa, Toronto CDSB

Katherine Shaw, Peel DSB

Jackie Stafford, Toronto DSB

Elizabeth Taylor, Peel DSB

Sian Thomas, Renfrew DSB

Elizabeth Thompson, Durham DSB

Bonnie Tkac-Feetham, Niagara CDSB

Sandra VandeCamp, Dufferin-Peel CDSB

Ann Varty, Trillium Lakelands DSB

Contents

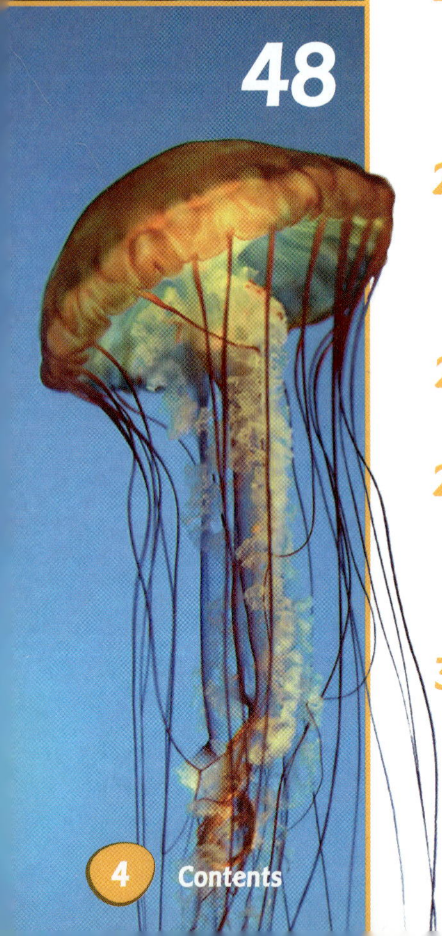

SOCIAL STUDIES

HEALTH

Welcome to

Nelson Literacy

Your *Nelson Literacy* book is full of fascinating stories and articles. Many of the topics are the same as those you will study in science, social studies, and health.

Here are the different kinds of pages you will see in this book:

Let's Talk

Here's a chance to have some fun and also show what you know.

Understanding Strategies

These pages introduce you to reading, writing, speaking, listening, and media literacy strategies. Some pages have sticky notes with hints about the strategies.

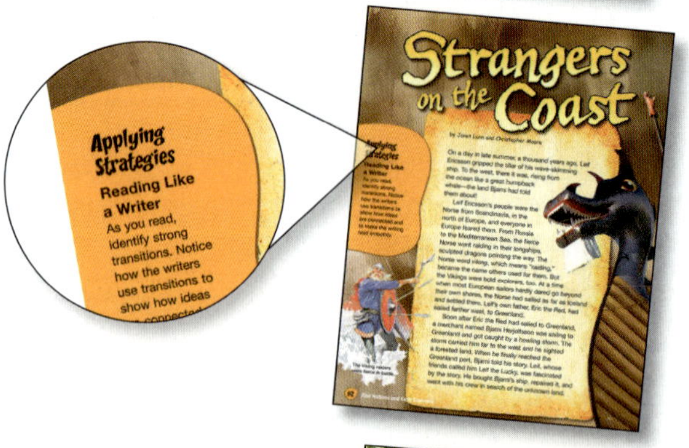

Applying Strategies

These pages give you the chance to try out the strategies you've learned.

Putting It All Together

At the end of each unit, you'll have the chance to use the strategies that you've learned.

Suspense

In this unit, you will

- activate prior knowledge
- identify characteristics of suspense stories
- acknowledge different points of view in conversations
- clarify ideas for writing
- identify purpose and audience for media texts

What Is Suspense?

Which of these situations would you find most suspenseful?
Which one would make for the best suspense story?

understanding reading strategies

Activating Prior Knowledge

Making connections helps you understand and enjoy what you are reading. You can use your prior knowledge to make connections. Think about your personal experiences, stories you have read or watched, and events happening in the world around you.

A BOY AND A MOUNTAIN

Written by James Ramsey Ullman
Illustrated by Carlos Martin Suaz

In the novel Banner in the Sky, *set in the year 1865, 16-year-old Rudi and his mother live in the Swiss Alps. Rudi loves to be in the mountains, but his mother disapproves. Rudi's father had been killed trying to climb the Citadel,* the unclimbable *mountain. She fears that her only son will die in the same way, but Rudi cannot stay away from the mountain that claimed his father's life. In this excerpt, Rudi learns of the mountain's dangers.*

Part 1

The Citadel rose up like a tower of iron. There was no movement anywhere. No stirring. No sound.

And then there was a sound....

Rudi stood motionless. It was not the sound of the mountain, of falling rock and ice. It was a voice. He waited; he looked around him; every sense was straining. But he saw nothing. Nothing moved. It was his imagination, he thought: a trick of his mind, or of the stillness. Or was it—and now the cold finger of fear touched him again—was it the voice of a mountain demon?

Think about your personal experiences. Do you know a family that has experienced a tragedy? How did it change their lives?

Think about your personal experiences. Have you ever felt so scared that your imagination started to play tricks on you?

He stood without breathing. And the sound came again. It seemed at the same time to come from nearby and far away. He waited. Once more it came. And then suddenly he knew *where* it came from. It was from beneath the ice. From a crevasse in the glacier.

He approached the nearest crevasse and called out. But there was no answer. He went on to a second. No answer. Again he waited and listened. Again the voice came, faintly. Straight ahead was a third chasm in the ice, and, advancing cautiously, he peered over the edge.

The crevasse was about two metres wide at the top and narrowed gradually as it went down. But how deep it was Rudi could not tell. After a few metres, the blue walls of ice curved away at a sharp slant, and what was below the curve was hidden from sight.

"Hello!" Rudi called.

"Hello—" A voice answered from the depths.

"How far down are you?"

"I'm not sure. About seven metres, I'd guess."

"On the bottom?"

"No, I can't even see the bottom. I was lucky and hit a ledge."

The voice spoke in German, but with a strange accent. Whoever was down there, Rudi knew, it was not one of the men of the valley.

"Are you hurt?" he called.

"Nothing broken—no," said the voice. "Just shaken up some. And cold."

"How long have you been there?"

"About three hours."

Rudi looked up and down the crevasse. He was thinking desperately of what he could do.

←

Think about events happening in the world around you. What accidents or disasters have you learned about by watching TV news? What problems did the victims face?

"Do you have a rope?" asked the voice.

"No."

"How many of you are there?"

"Only me."

There was a silence. When the voice spoke again, it was still quiet and under strict control. "Then you'll have to go for help," it said.

Rudi didn't answer. To get down to Kurtal would take at least two hours, and for a party to climb back up would take three. By that time it would be night, and the man would have been in the crevasse for eight hours. He would be frozen to death.

"No," said Rudi, "it would take too long."

"What else is there to do?"

Rudi's eyes moved over the ice walls: almost vertical, smooth as glass. "Have you an axe?" he asked.

"No. I lost it when I fell. It dropped to the bottom."

"Have you tried to climb?"

"Yes. But I can't get a hold."

There was another silence. Rudi's lips tightened, and when he spoke again his voice was strained. "I'll think of something," he cried. "I'll think of *something!*"

"Don't lose your head," the voice said. "The only way is to go down for help."

"But you'll—"

"Maybe. And maybe not. That's a chance we'll have to take."

The voice was as quiet as ever. And, hearing it, Rudi was suddenly ashamed. Here was he, safe on the glacier's surface, showing fear and despair, while the one below, facing almost certain death, remained calm and controlled. Whoever it was down there, it was a very brave man.

Think about stories you have read or watched. What characters do you know who were very brave?

Rudi drew in a long, slow breath. With his climbing staff he felt down along the smooth surface of the ice walls.

"Are you still there?" said the voice.

"Yes," he said.

"You had better go."

"Wait—"

Lying flat on the glacier, he leaned over the rim of the crevasse and lowered the staff as far as it would go. Its end came almost to the curve of the walls.

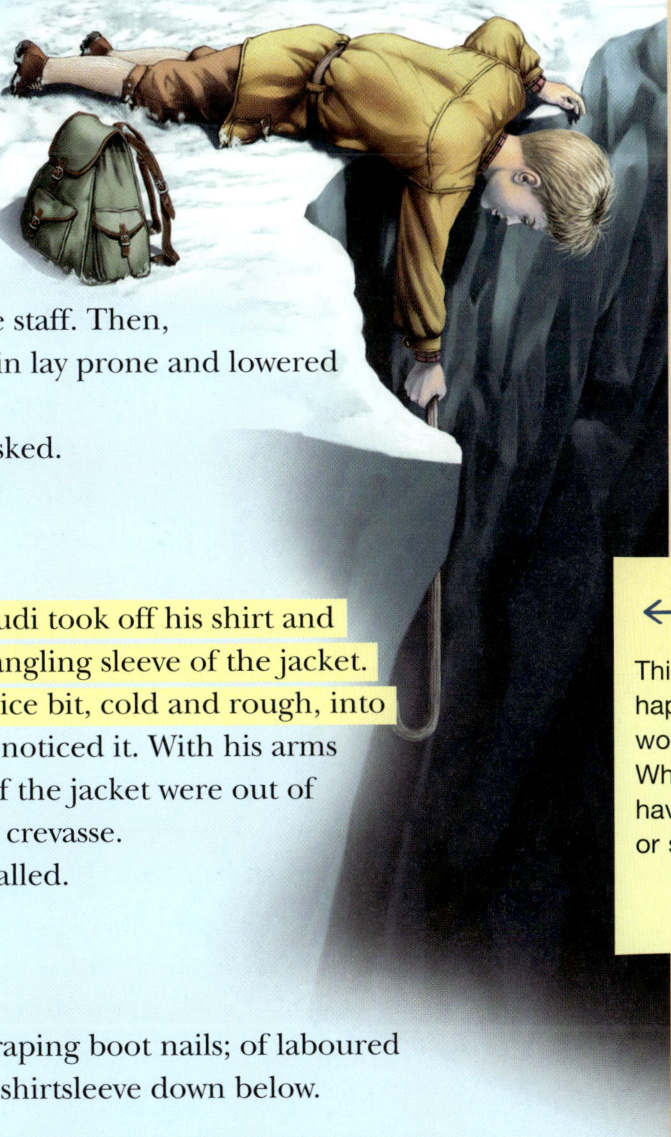

"Can you see it?" he asked.

"See what?" said the man.

Obviously he couldn't. Standing up, Rudi removed his jacket and tied it by one sleeve to the curved end of the staff. Then, holding the other end, he again lay prone and lowered his staff and jacket.

"Can you see it now?" he asked.

"Yes," said the man.

"How far above you is it?"

"About three metres."

Again the staff came up. Rudi took off his shirt and tied one of its sleeves to the dangling sleeve of the jacket. This time, as he lay down, the ice bit, cold and rough, into his bare chest; but he scarcely noticed it. With his arms extended, all the shirt and half the jacket were out of sight beneath the curve in the crevasse.

"How near you now?" he called.

"Not far," said the voice.

"Can you reach it?"

"I'm trying."

There was the sound of scraping boot nails; of laboured breathing. But no pull on the shirtsleeve down below.

←

Think about events happening in the world around you. What daring rescues have you read about or seen on TV?

A Boy and a Mountain

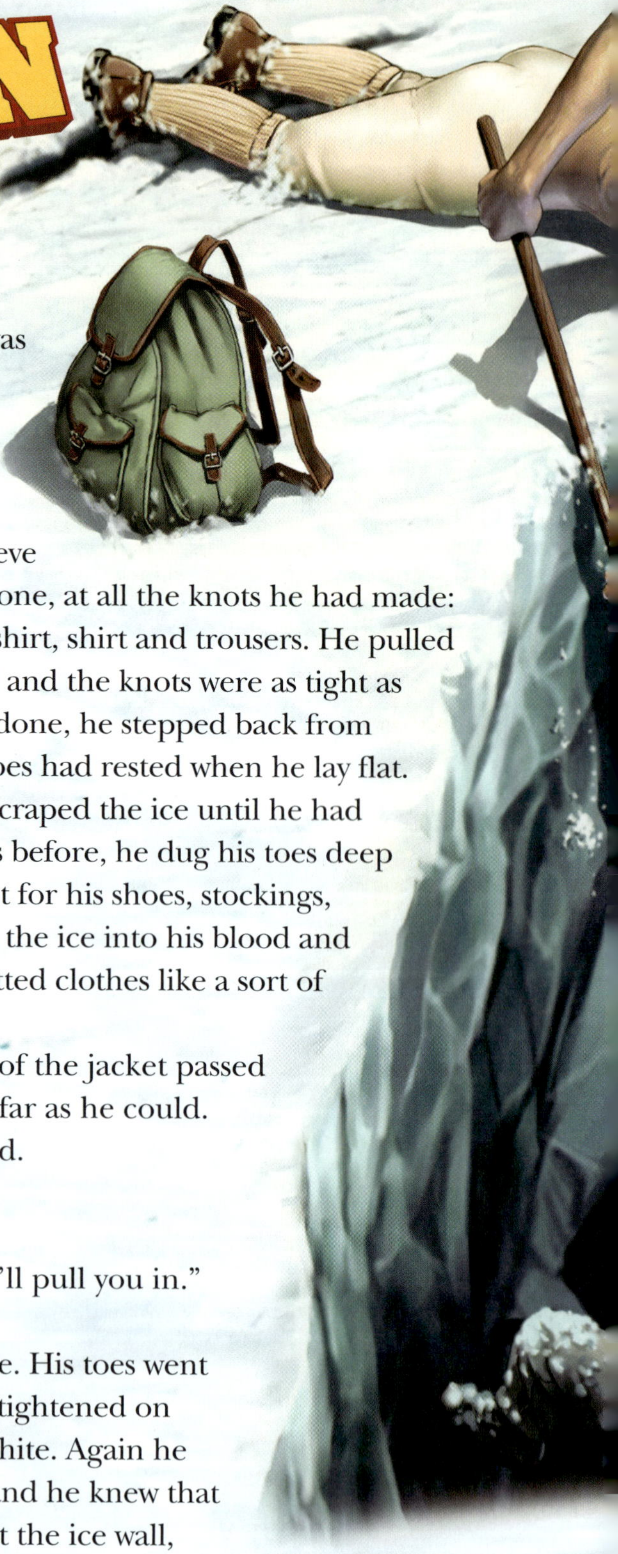

Part 2

"I can't make it," said the voice. It was fainter than before.

"Wait," said Rudi.

For the third time, he raised the staff. He took off his trousers. He tied a trouser leg to the loose sleeve of the shirt. Then he pulled, one by one, at all the knots he had made: between staff and jacket, jacket and shirt, shirt and trousers. He pulled until the blood pounded in his head and the knots were as tight as his strength could make them. This done, he stepped back from the crevasse to the point where his toes had rested when he lay flat. With feet and hands he kicked and scraped the ice until he had made two holes. Then, lying down as before, he dug his toes deep into them. He was naked now, except for his shoes, stockings, and underpants. The cold rose from the ice into his blood and bones. He lowered the staff and knotted clothes like a sort of crazy fishing line.

The trousers, the shirt, and half of the jacket passed out of sight. He was leaning over as far as he could.

"Can you reach it now?" he called.

"Yes," the voice answered.

"All right. Come on."

"You won't be able to hold me. I'll pull you in."

"No, you won't."

He braced himself. The pull came. His toes went taut in their ice holds and his hands tightened on the staff until the knuckles showed white. Again he could hear a scraping sound below, and he knew that the man was clawing his boots against the ice wall, trying to lever himself up and to take as much weight as possible off the improvised lifeline. But the wall obviously offered little help. Almost all his weight was on the lifeline. Suddenly there was a jerk, as one of

Applying Strategies

Activating Prior Knowledge

As you read, activate your prior knowledge to help you make connections.

- Think about your personal experiences.
- Think about stories you have read or watched.
- Think about events happening in the world around you.

the knots in the clothing slipped, and the staff was almost wrenched from Rudi's hands. But the knot held. And his hands held. He tried to call down, "All right?" but he had no breath for words. From below, the only sound was the scraping of boots on ice.

How long it went on Rudi could never have said. Perhaps only for a minute or so. But it seemed like hours. And then—at last—it happened. A hand came into view around the curve of the crevasse wall: a hand gripping the twisted fabric of his jacket, and then a second hand rising slowly above it. A head appeared. A pair of shoulders. A face was raised for an instant and then lowered. Again one hand moved slowly up past the other.

But Rudi no longer saw it, for now his eyes were shut tight with the strain. His teeth were clamped, the cords of his neck bulged, the muscles of his arm felt as if they were being drawn one by one from the bones that held them. He began to lose his toeholds. He was being dragged forward. Desperately, frantically, he dug in with his feet, pressed his whole body down, as if he could make it part of the glacier. Though all but naked on the ice, he was pouring with sweat. Somehow he stopped the slipping. Somehow he held on. But now, suddenly, the strain was even worse, for the man had reached the lower end of the staff. The slight "give" of the stretched clothing was gone, and in its place was rigid dead weight on a length of wood. The climber was close now. But heavy. Indescribably heavy. Rudi's hands ached and burned, as if it were a rod of hot lead that they clung to. It was not a mere man he was holding, but a giant, or a block of granite. The pull was unendurable. The pain unendurable. He could hold on no longer. His hands were opening. It was all over.

And then it *was* over. The weight was gone. There was a scraping sound close beneath him; a hand on the rim of ice; a figure pulling itself up onto the lip of the crevasse. The man was beside Rudi, turning to him, staring at him.

"Why—you're just a boy!" he said in astonishment.

Rudi was too numb to move or speak. Taking the staff from him, the man pulled up the line of clothes, untied the knots, and shook them out.

"Come on now. Quickly!" he said.

Pulling the boy to his feet, he helped him dress. Then he rubbed and pummelled him until at last Rudi felt the warmth of returning circulation.

"Better?" the man asked, smiling.

Rudi nodded. And finally he was able to speak again. "And you, sir," he said, "you are all right?"

The man nodded. He was warming himself now: flapping his arms and kicking his feet together. "A few minutes of sun and I'll be as good as new."

Nearby, a black boulder lay embedded in the glacial ice, and, going over to it, they sat down. The sunlight poured over them like a warm bath. Rudi slowly flexed his aching fingers and saw that the man was doing the same. And then the man had raised his eyes and was looking at him.

"It's a miracle how you did it," he said. "A boy of your size. All alone."

"It was nothing," Rudi murmured.

"Nothing?"

"I—I only—"

"Only saved my life," said the man.

For the first time, now, Rudi was really seeing him. He was a man of perhaps 30, very tall and thin, and his face, too, was thin, with a big hawklike nose and a strong, jutting chin. His weather-browned cheeks were cleanshaven, his hair black, his eyes deep-set and grey. And when he spoke, his voice was still almost as quiet as when it had been muffled by the ice walls of the crevasse. He is—what—Rudi thought. Not Swiss, he knew. Not French or German. English, perhaps? Yes, English.... And then suddenly a deep excitement filled him, for he knew who the man was.

"You are Captain Winter?" he murmured.

"That's right."

"And I—I have saved—I mean—"

Rudi was wordless—almost stunned. He looked at the man, and then away in embarrassment, and he could scarcely believe what had happened. The name of Captain John Winter was known through the length and breadth of the Alps. He was the foremost mountaineer of his day, and during the past 10 years had made more first ascents of great peaks than any other person alive. Rudi had heard that he had come to Kurtal a few days before. He had hoped that at least he would see him in the hotel or walking by in the street. But actually to meet him—and in this way! To pull him from a crevasse—save him.... It was incredible!

Reflect on

Strategies: Find a place where you made a very strong connection to the story. How did the connection help you understand the story?

Critical Literacy: Imagine that the story of Rudi's rescue of Captain Winter travels from the mountain to Rudi's village to TV news. What would different people emphasize? What would they leave out?

Understanding speaking and listening strategies

Acknowledging Different Points of View

The most interesting discussions are ones where there are several different points of view. To enjoy a lively discussion, you need to be both a good listener and a good speaker.

These student council members are meeting to recommend a movie for Grades 4, 5, and 6 to watch on the upcoming special activities day. Not surprisingly, there's some disagreement!

How to acknowledge different points of view:

- ✔ Be an active listener. Ask questions to help you understand each person's point of view.
- ✔ Point out something you learned or agree with in someone else's point of view.
- ✔ Explain why you think the way you do.

Understanding media

Identifying Purpose and Audience

Thrills and Chills

Would you like to fill your Saturday afternoon with thrills and chills? You could try a book or a movie. But how will you decide? Film studios and publishers use movie posters and book covers to try to get your attention. The purpose of these media texts is to find and create an audience.

An interesting design, or "look," attracts attention. Who do you think is the audience for this book? How do this image and title work together to attract viewers?

A strong image draws viewers in and makes them want to know more. What audience might stop to look at this image? What questions would viewers be asking?

Additional information reaches out to the largest possible audience. Why do you think the author's name is at the top of the cover? Why is the name of another book given?

Look at this poster for the movie *A Series of Unfortunate Events*. How do the design, the image, and the additional information reach out to attract an audience for the movie? Is this movie poster trying to attract the same audience as the one for *Nightmare Mountain*, or a different audience?

Understanding text patterns

Narrative: Identifying Characteristics of Suspense Stories

Suspense stories have certain characteristics:

- The characters fear something very bad is about to happen.
- A character or situation poses a real threat.
- Something very important is at stake, or threatened.
- Events are fast paced and tension builds throughout the story.

The characters fear something very bad is about to happen. Why is Joanna afraid? How do you know?

A VISIT FROM THE SLAVE CATCHER

Written by Barbara Greenwood Illustrated by Anton Petrov

In the 1800s, American slave catchers sometimes crossed the border to kidnap slaves who had escaped to freedom in Canada. The slave catchers hoped for a reward when they returned the slaves to their American owners. In this excerpt from the novel A Parcel for Joanna, *a young girl named Melanie has escaped slavery and made her way to St. Catharines, Ontario. Melanie is being sheltered by Joanna Reid's family until her mother arrives. One day, while Joanna's parents are away from the house, a stranger appears at the door.*

Part 1

Humming happily, Joanna clattered mugs and muffin tins onto the kitchen table and was reaching for the kettle when a movement outside caught her eye. A slim shape flitted furtively past the window. Then suddenly it was back, and a face peered in at her. Joanna felt her heart lurch into her mouth as the face grinned and disappeared. Who was it? In the distorting bubbled glass she had caught only an impression....

It doesn't matter who. I mustn't open the door to anyone while we're alone. As a precaution, she flew toward the inside bolt—but she was too late. The handle turned and the door swung inward. The stranger she had seen in the shop that morning stepped politely into the kitchen.

"Yes?" she asked breathlessly, standing close to the doorway so that he would have to stop or push her aside. "What do you want?"

"Afternoon, missy." A thin-lipped smile stretched his stubbly cheeks. "Got some real good news for your little guest."

"Melanie?" Joanna exclaimed, and then could have bitten her tongue. Did she imagine it or were his eyes glinting in triumph?

"The very one." He smiled broadly, showing yellow teeth. "Got a message from her ma," he said, raising his voice and craning his neck to see around Joanna, who stood firm. "She's safe here in Canada and she wants her little girl to come right away so they can take the steamer to Toronto."

Joanna frowned. "Why didn't you tell my father that this morning?"

←

A character or situation poses a real threat. How did the stranger outsmart Joanna?

He raised his eyebrows and shrugged. "Didn't know the little lady existed this morning. Just met my good friend Abram Fuller on the road. Soon's I heard what he was about, I said, 'Don't you worry. I'll be right in that neighbourhood. Seein' as how y're a busy man, I'll pass on the joyful news and bring the little girl out meself.'" He grinned at her again. "Now you just fetch your little friend and we'll be on our way."

Joanna felt confused. Should she believe him? Everything about him made her wary. "Never judge a parcel by its wrappings," her mother always said. But it wasn't just his dirty hands and scruffy appearance that bothered her.

"Hurry up, now! I ain't got all day."

The sharp demand rattled her so that she half-turned to the bedroom to call Melanie. Instantly he stopped acting friendly and pushed past her into the room. Panic-stricken, she retreated further.

"You're mistaken," she gasped. "There's no one else here."

The stranger's face flushed with rage. "You fetch me that girl," he hissed. "Now!"

Terrified, Joanna turned to run, but he reached out and caught her wrist. She twisted wildly and bit the hand that held her.

→

Something very important is at stake, or threatened. What does the stranger want?

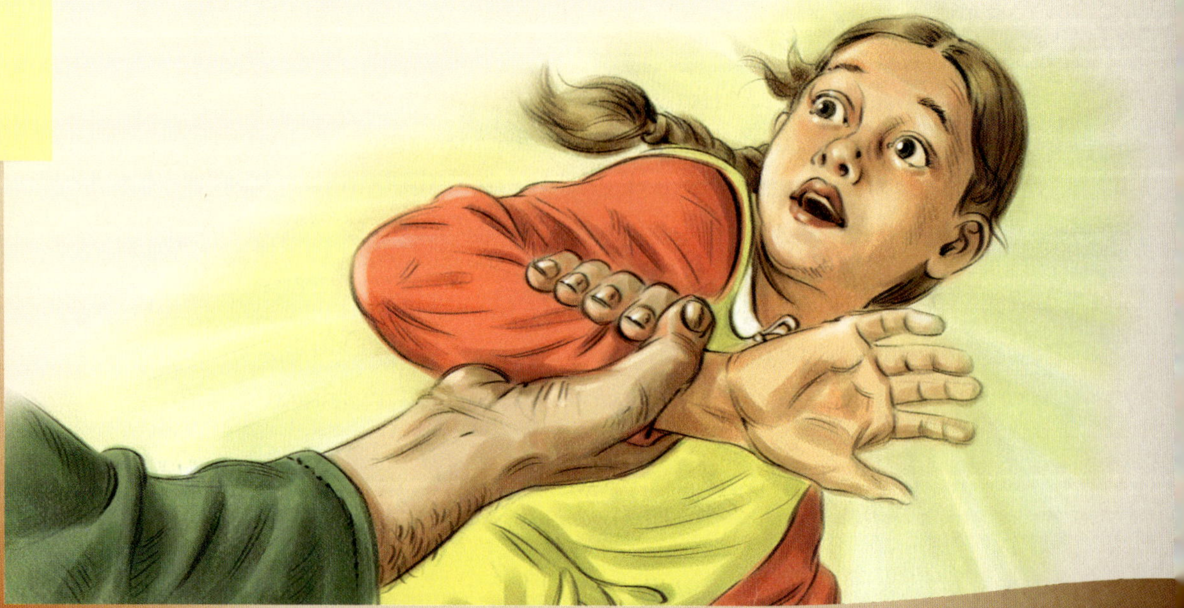

"Thunderation!" He spat venomously and let go just as a living tornado swept out of the bedroom. Head down, Melanie charged full-tilt into the stranger and knocked him off balance. He staggered backward, tripped on the doorstep, and fell sprawling on the porch. Joanna jumped for the door, slammed it shut, and shot all the bolts.

Weak with relief, the girls stared at each other.

"The slave catcher?"

Melanie nodded.

"How did you know?"

Melanie shrugged. "Had a feelin'. I just know 'bout folks like that. Anyway, what call has Mr. Fuller got to send him here? He knows your daddy's bringin' him barrels today. And if my mama was in Queenston, she'd never send the likes of that one to come and fetch me."

Joanna sat down limply but Melanie still stood, frowning, in the middle of the room. "What's he at now?" she asked, listening tensely to the silence.

Joanna tiptoed to the window. To her horror, the slave catcher was standing in the yard, hands on hips, staring thoughtfully at the roof, then along the side of the house.

Events are fast paced and tension builds throughout the story. Why is Joanna horrified when she looks out the window?

←

A VISIT FROM THE SLAVE CATCHER

Part 2

Applying Strategies

Narrative: Identifying Characteristics of Suspense Stories

As you read, identify the characteristics of suspense stories:

- The characters fear something very bad is about to happen.
- A character or situation poses a real threat.
- Something very important is at stake, or threatened.
- Events are fast paced and tension builds throughout the story.

"He's not going away," Joanna said, half-turning to Melanie. But when she looked back, he had vanished. Where had he gone? Anxiously she imagined him prowling around the house, looking, looking. There was no way in at the back. The lean-to that ran across the back of the house and shop had only one very small window. There was another window along the side of the shop. Surely he wouldn't dare try the front door. Anyway, it was locked—wasn't it? She raced into the parlour, Melanie at her heels.

Yes, the door, which opened directly into the front parlour, was locked. As an added precaution, Joanna shot the bolts, then checked the door that led from the back parlour out to the lean-to.

As she latched it firmly, she said, "Perhaps we should make a run for it. Mother's just down the street. The neighbours might hear us if we screamed." And then again, they mightn't, she thought, remembering how far apart houses were here on the outskirts of St. Catharines.

Just then Melanie clutched at her and pointed. A shadow was passing in front of the window. The front door handle rattled briefly, then the shadow passed in front of the next window.

"He's circling the house!" Joanna whispered. "Listen, Melanie, as soon as he's around the back, we'll make a run for it."

"How'll you know when he's around the back? What if he's crouched out there ready to pounce on us?"

The girls looked at each other in despair.

"Surely Mama can't be much longer!"

"Better if we just wait right here. Long as he's outside, we're safe inside."

"Sh!" Joanna said. "What was that?"

From somewhere had come the tinkle of breaking glass. The girls stood rigid, straining to hear. Their own heartbeats seemed to echo through the silent house. A sudden thud made them start convulsively. Then a door hinge creaked.

"He must have broken into the shop," Joanna gasped, as she guessed where the sounds came from. Then a loud crash and a sharp oath exploding into the silence told her the stranger had stumbled over something in the dark lean-to. Now only the flimsy back parlour door with its hook-and-eye latch barred the slave catcher's way.

"We've *got* to run for it!" Joanna gasped, but Melanie was already tugging frantically at the lower bolt of the front door.

Joanna flew at the upper one, willing her mind to concentrate, to blot out the sounds of the blows that were shattering the back parlour door. With a sudden lurch the bolt yielded. Now the key. Just as the teeth of the big key tripped the tumblers of the lock, the back door splintered open.

"Run, run!" Joanna screamed, pushing Melanie out in front of her. As they sped down the front steps, Joanna felt a hand on her shoulder, twisted from under it, and darted after Melanie. They turned down the road. Joanna spurted ahead, leading the way toward neighbours, toward Mother. Suddenly Melanie stumbled in a wagon rut and fell.

Joanna heard a triumphant "Gotcha!" and whirled around as the slave catcher dragged Melanie roughly to her feet. Fear turned to fury. With a shriek of rage she threw herself at the man, pummelling him with her fists.

"Let go. Let go. Let go!" Then suddenly he was plucked away and the girls were left clutching each other.

As her wild heartbeats calmed, Joanna raised her head and looked around. At the side of the road was her father's wagon and team. In the centre of an excited knot of neighbours, firmly grasping the slave catcher, was her father. The crowd fell silent. Mr. Reid, clutching his captive by the lapels of his coat, and deliberately shaking him for emphasis, was almost whispering in repressed rage.

"Listen, my friend … in this town we don't take kindly … to anyone terrorizing … our children. Neither … do we like vermin … who traffic … in the slave trade. If you value your hide … you won't show your face … on this side of the river … again!"

Then there was a flurry among the watchers, and two mothers swooped down on two daughters to hug, and scold, and cry.

"Mama!" Melanie cried. "Look, Joanna. Here's my mama safe at last."

Reflect on

Strategies: List three or four events that show how the girls' situation is moving from bad to worse. Why do the events create a feeling of suspense in the reader?

Your Learning: You've probably learned about how Canadians helped American slaves escape to freedom in Canada in the 1800s. How does reading a suspenseful story about this time add to your understanding?

Understanding writing strategies

Clarifying Ideas

We often talk about how it's important for writers to "hook" readers—to get them interested so they'll want to keep reading right to the end. But writers need to be hooked, too! Being excited about your idea for a story is the first step to writing a great story.

This writer wants to write a suspense story, but she's not sure how to get started. She decides to do some sketching to clarify her ideas.

How to clarify ideas:

- ☑ Think of several ideas and try to visualize each one.
- ☑ Draw a quick sketch of the idea that gave you the strongest picture in your mind.
- ☑ Give your sketch a title.
- ☑ Add details in pictures and words.

Applying Strategies

Reading Like a Writer

As you read, identify the writer's idea. Locate details that help you see the events clearly in your mind.

The Quecreek Mine Disaster

by Larry Verstraete

On that day—Wednesday, July 24, 2002—Mark Popernack and Thomas Foy were the first of the nine miners to know that something was horribly wrong.

The miners were deep within Pennsylvania's Quecreek Mine, inside one of many passageways that riddled the coal mine. The men had worked together for years. They were close, like brothers, and that day they were nearing the end of their shift.

Popernack operated the continuous miner, a grinding machine with a spinning head resembling a giant corncob with hundreds of steel teeth. The machine crunched forward, chipping rock loose, steadily expanding the tunnel.

Maps showed the rock was 100 m thick, far away from other mining shafts and tunnels. It was safe to go ahead, the men were told—as safe as work in a deep mine can ever be.

At 8:45 p.m., a plug of rock loosened, popping out like a cork. A torrent of water spilled from the hole, washing over Popernack's machine.

A Map of the Mines

This simplified diagram shows Quecreek Mine and the abandoned mine. No one realized how close the abandoned mine was to a tunnel in Quecreek Mine.

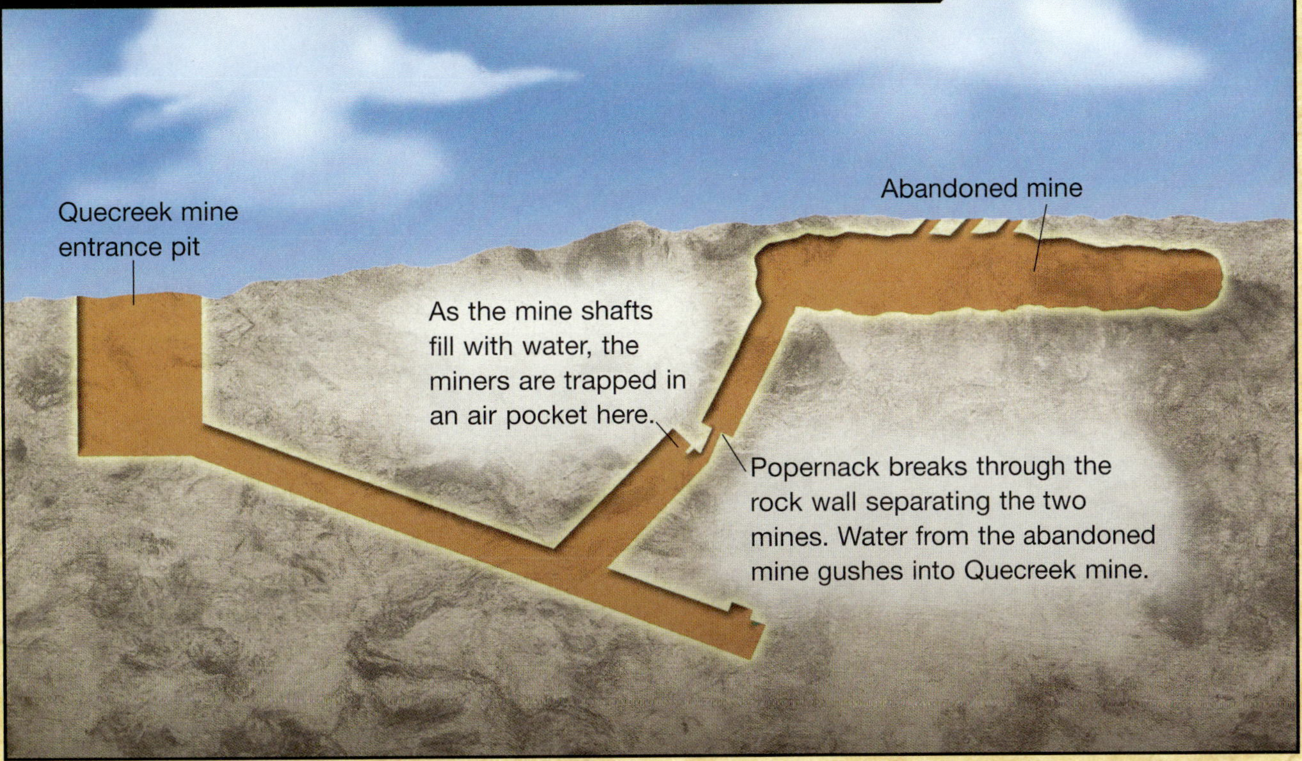

The maps had been wrong. An old, abandoned mine was on the other side of the wall, much closer than anyone had thought. Over decades, water had seeped into the mine. The continuous miner had chewed through the wall, starting a flood in the tunnel.

"Everyone out!" screamed Foy, who was working nearby.

Popernack leaped from the miner machine, springing to the rocks on the opposite side of the rising water, safe but now separated from the other men. One man raced to a mine phone to warn a second crew working in a lower section of the mine.

Forced to leave Popernack behind, the eight miners sloshed through the rising water, fighting to stay on their feet. They were heading to a conveyor belt that moved coal out of the shaft. The conveyor was dead, its power cut by the water, but they hopped on it anyway, clambering and tripping over the coal on the conveyor belt as they raced to stay ahead of the water.

But by the light of their headlamps, they soon saw that the water had already won the race. It had entered the tunnel ahead through side passages, filling it to the ceiling in places.

The men reversed direction, clinging to the conveyor. Water swirled around their chins as they fought to reach safety. Now and then, they veered into other passageways, hoping to find one better than their own. But there was no escaping the water. It was everywhere.

• • •

On the surface, the second crew emerged from the mine and alerted rescuers. If the nine miners were still alive, they would be trying to reach higher ground, rescuers figured. Using global positioning satellites and maps of the mine, they pinpointed a site where they thought the miners would go.

Government officials and rescue workers come up with a plan for getting the trapped miners out.

Quickly, a bold and ambitious plan was hatched. First they would drill two shafts—send an air pipe down one and pump out water from the other. Then, depending on where the men were (and if they were still alive by then), they would bore another hole wider than the others—an escape tunnel!

There was much to do: locate equipment (build it if necessary), set up drilling rigs and pumps, organize crews, alert medical workers, notify families ... and drill.

Boring holes through 75 m of rock would take time. And time was running out.

• • •

Popernack was trapped and alone. Suddenly he spotted a light across the water. The other men had come back.

"Get me over with you guys!" Popernack shouted.

A mechanical scoop was edged into the swirling water, its bucket raised high. "Jump!" Popernack was told. He leaped into the bucket and was eased to the other side. The men were together, all nine, like brothers again.

They found an air pocket close to the conveyor, near several other smaller passageways, all of them gushing water. To slow the water, the men stacked cement blocks in front of the passages.

They waited, fighting the cold and the foul, dank air. In the distance, they heard drilling. Help was coming—wasn't it?

On Thursday at 5:10 a.m., nine hours after the flood had begun, a 10 cm pipe dropped through the ceiling near the conveyor. An air shaft! The first sign that help was on its way.

Quickly, the miners pounded on the pipe, sending a message to the surface—nine bangs to say, "Nine men alive."

Shouts and cheers erupted on the surface. The miners had been found! To provide oxygen and warmth, and to help stop the rising water, heated compressed air was forced down the pipe.

Then, on Thursday at 7:30 p.m., the escape tunnel was started. A super-sized drill bit had been hauled by helicopter to the site and fastened to a specialized drilling rig. The bit slowly ground through the rock, chewing a hole big enough to fit a man. It would take at least 15 hours to reach the miners. Could they hang on that long?

• • •

Down below, the water continued to rise. The miners retreated to higher ground. They had an hour, they figured, before the water reached them.

They wrote notes to their families on snippets of cardboard, placed them in a bucket and lashed it to a boulder. Then they looped steel cable through their belts, tethering the nine men together. This way their bodies wouldn't be scattered through the mine. If they had to die, they would do it together.

To conserve power, they switched off their helmet lamps and huddled together in the darkness to keep each other warm. The water level seemed to be dropping now, and they could hear more drilling. Rescuers were coming, they were sure. It was just a matter of time.

Then on Friday at 1:50 a.m. the drilling stopped.

• • •

Rescuers work around the clock to prepare equipment.

Partway down, the bit had broken, stalling the rescue and eating up precious time. The bit had to be removed, but the job required a specially made tool. Workers in an ironworks plant flew into action, constructing the device in just three hours.

By Friday at 8:00 p.m. the broken bit was out and drilling on the shaft resumed.

• • •

The rescue capsule is unloaded at the site.

Surrounded by silence, the men talked, sharing memories, discussing ambitions—anything to keep their spirits up.

Hours later, the sound of drilling finally resumed, rekindling hopes of rescue. Every 15 minutes, someone sloshed down the tunnel to the air shaft to pound a message on the pipe: Nine bangs—nine men still alive.

Late on Saturday night, two miners made a discovery. They raced back to the others screaming the news. "We found the hole!"

The other miners bolted down the tunnel, anxious to see for themselves. It was there all right. A hole big enough to fit a man, punched right through the ceiling.

Rescue workers react with joy after making voice contact with the trapped miners.

From the hole, a phone line appeared.

"Are you the trapped miners?" a voice said.

"Yes, we are," they answered.

"How many are you?"

"We're all nine here," came the reply.

The joyous news spread like wildfire, to dozens of rescue workers nearby, to families anxiously waiting, to reporters and television crews who'd swarmed the site.

A rescue capsule was lowered down the shaft. One by one, the men were hauled to the surface, weak and blackened with coal dust, but grateful to be alive. After 77 hours in the mine, the nine miners were safe, united once again, brothers to the end.

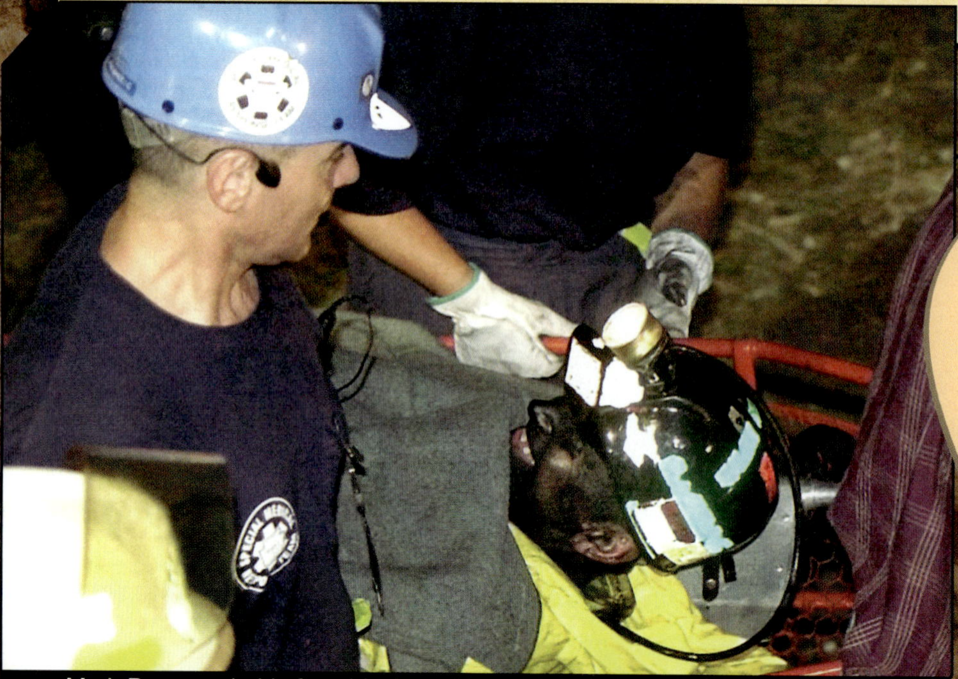
Mark Popernack, his face blackened by coal dust, is carried to a waiting ambulance.

Reflect on

Writer's Craft: How did focusing on the trapped Quecreek miners help to make Larry Verstraete's ideas clear? What stories did he leave out?

Connections: Think of a TV show or news program about a disaster or a daring rescue. How was that story like the one you've just read? How was it different?

Akla Gives Chase

Written and illustrated by James Houston

Putting It All Together

As you read, remember to use the strategies you've learned in this unit:

- Activate prior knowledge.
- Think about the characteristics of suspense stories.
- Recognize how the writer clarified ideas.

Upik and Pitohok are two Inuit children who live in Canada's Far North. Their father has died and the family has run out of food. It is up to the two children to make the long journey to retrieve a caribou their grandfather had killed and hidden earlier. Without this precious source of food, the family will starve.

Weak from hunger and exhausted by their long journey, Upik and Pitohok struggle back with the heavy caribou. But they are pursued by Long Claws—an "akla," or grizzly bear. Finally they believe they have escaped from the bear and can make their way home hidden by thick, icy fog.

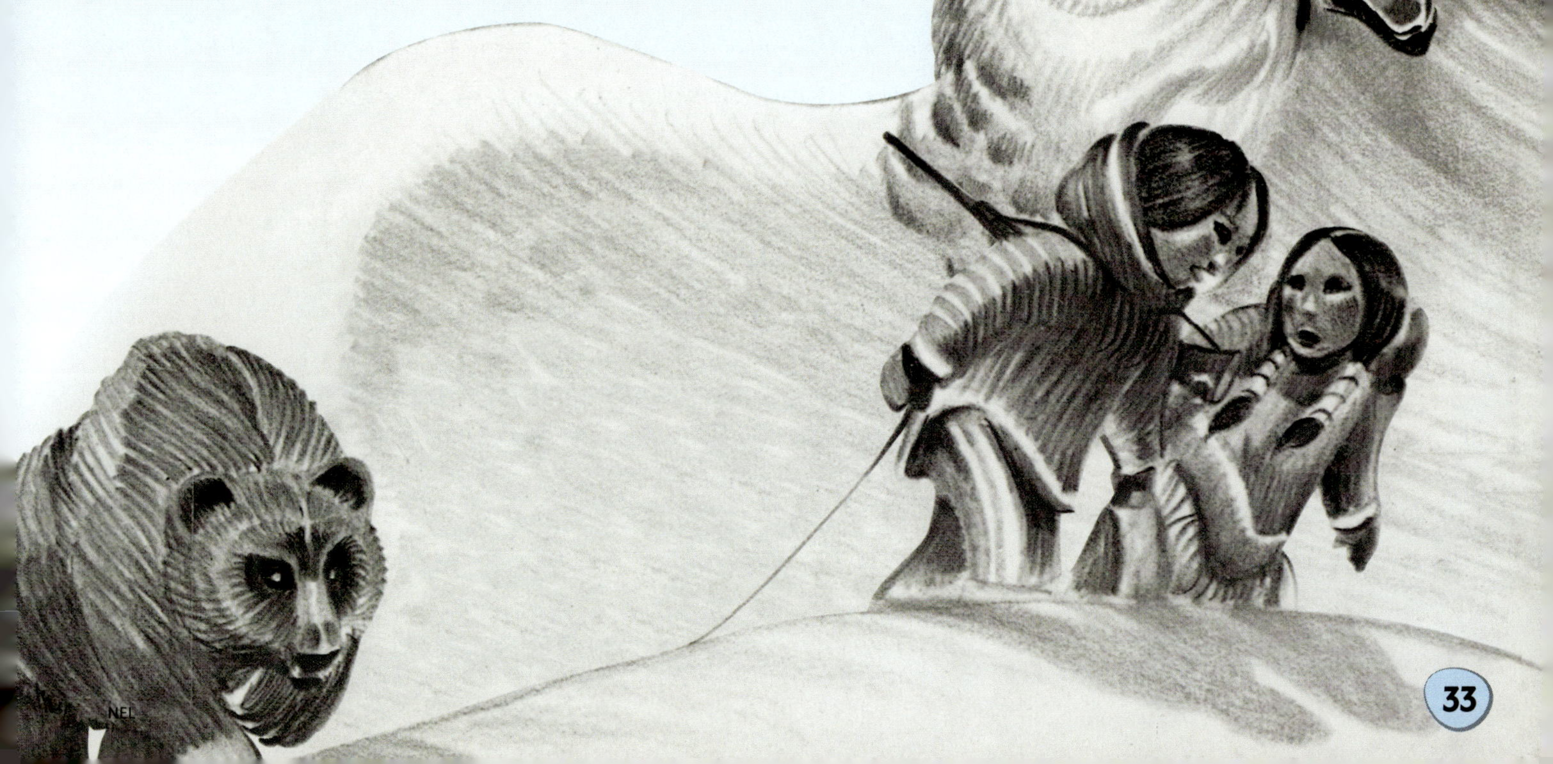

"I hope we are far enough away from him," Pitohok gasped. "I can walk no farther."

He sank to his knees and let the heavy weight of the caribou sag down until it rested on the wind-cleared stones. He lay against it, his chest heaving as he tried to catch his breath. Although the air was stinging cold, Upik had to kneel and wipe the frost-white sweat from her brother's face.

"He's gone." Upik sighed, glad to rest the heavy rifle in the snow. She looked around in the still-thick fog. "Which way do we go now?"

Pitohok peered over his shoulder and felt cold sweat trickling down his spine. He could see no sign of the sun. Everything was hidden by a wall of fog.

"I … I don't know," he admitted. "I was trying so hard to get away from the akla that now … we're lost!"

Pitohok struggled painfully onto his knees and looked in all directions. He saw nothing but grey ice fog that drifted in phantom swirls along the frozen river.

"Oh, I wish someone would help us," Upik whispered aloud, and as if in answer to her words, the snowy owl came toward her, winging low out of the fog. Upik saw the owl turn its head as though it had seen the bear, then stare at her with its huge golden-yellow eyes. Suddenly the owl changed its wingbeat, hovering as if by magic at the very edge of the smokelike mists. It seemed to signal Upik. Then, turning sharply to the right, it flew off, cutting a dark trail through the ice-cold wall of fog.

Upik stood up and, using all her strength, helped her brother heave the caribou onto his back. She struggled to ease the heavy burden as she stood upright.

"We should follow her," said Upik. "I think she knows the way."

Her brother's answer was a moan when the full weight of the frozen caribou settled on his tired, cramped shoulders. "Yes, follow the owl," he whispered.

Upik tried to steady Pitohok while they walked. She looked back only once at the zigzag trail they left in the snow as her brother's strength grew less and less. Both of them had lost all sense of distance and of time. Upik followed the owl's course through the dense fog, wondering if they would ever reach their home.

They had not gone far before Upik heard the sound of heavy breathing. She turned, then screamed in terror. The huge grizzly, its heavy head rolling, its tongue lolling out of its mouth, came padding after them. It was only a pace behind Pitohok. Upik saw Long Claws raise its head and sniff at the rich burden of caribou, which had softened a little because of the heat of Pitohok's body. The grizzly stretched out its neck and licked the frosted nostrils of the caribou.

"What's the matter?" Pitohok asked her. Then, turning, he too saw the bear. His voice caught in his throat. "You've got to … to try and shoot him," Pitohok gasped. "I can't do it. My arms are too tired. My whole body is trembling from carrying this weight. Let him get close to you," he said, "then shoot him … in the head."

Upik stopped, raised the heavy rifle and tried to sight along its wavering barrel. "I can't," she said. "I am afraid … afraid this last stone bullet will break." She was weeping. "Drop the caribou," Upik begged her brother. "Let Long Claws take it. We can walk away alive. It will stop and eat. Please drop the caribou. I am afraid that the akla is going to kill you for that meat."

Pitohok hunched his shoulders and struggled forward, as if he had not heard her plea. But now Upik could see that he held his short knife in his hand and that he would not give up their prize of meat without a fight.

Once more she heard an angry rumble in the grizzly's throat and saw it reach out with one terrible paw and rake the caribou along the whole length of its back. As its claws hooked against the caribou's antlers, Pitohok was thrown off balance and stumbled sideways, falling onto his knees. The big bear moved closer. Driven by fear and desperation, Pitohok rose and continued walking, his eyes narrowed, his mouth drawn down with strain.

The huge akla, with lips drawn back to show its enormous teeth, came after him again. Upik once more raised her grandfather's rifle and looked along its sights. The bear must have heard the safety catch click off, for it stopped, turned its head, and stared straight up the gun barrel at her. At that moment, looking into its eyes, Upik realized that the bear was neither good nor evil. It was a hunter like themselves, desperate to feed itself and remain alive in the lonely, snow-filled wilderness. She lowered the rifle. She could not bring herself to try to kill the bear.

At that moment, Pitohok whispered hoarsely, "I see the owl again! She's sitting on our family's empty food cache. Can it be?" he sobbed. "Are we … almost home?"

The bear moved in again behind him and, raising up on its hind feet, struck out angrily at the caribou's plump haunches. Pitohok reeled from the heavy blow and staggered to his knees. He tried to rise, then sank back onto the snow.

"I can't go on," he said. "I'm finished." He had lost his knife. There were tears in his eyes, but his teeth were clenched in anger. He tightened his grip upon the caribou.

"Let go," Upik begged her brother. "Let him have the meat."

"No," Pitohok said. "If I lose this caribou to that bear and return home with nothing, none of us will live, and I, myself, would die of shame."

He turned away from the hot breath of the snarling grizzly whose great swaying head was not more than an arm's length from his face.

"Run!" Pitohok whispered to his sister. "Run for the igloo and save yourself."

Upik bent and grabbed her brother underneath the arms, trying to help him up, but he was too weak. Then she turned around so that she stood directly between him and the akla's gaping jaws.

"No—don't do that," Pitohok gasped. He was hunched over like an old man. "Put the rifle under the caribou to help me support this weight," he moaned, "or I ... shall never rise. You run!" he begged his sister. Pitohok wept aloud as he whispered, "I can't do any more. All my strength has gone. It's going black ... I'm going to...."

"You are coming with me, now!" cried Upik. "I can see our igloo. It's not far from us. Can you not see it through the fog?"

The big grizzly raked its claws through the snow. Upik put her left shoulder underneath the caribou and her arm around her brother's waist and strained with all her might. Together they rose from the snow and staggered off toward their family's house. Pitohok stumbled once again and fell onto one knee. He hung there, gasping for breath.

The akla snarled and opened its mouth wide to take the caribou's leg and Pitohok's mitted hand between its crushing jaws.

"Unalook! Kukikotak!" Upik screamed at the bear. "We shared our fish with you. Don't you dare to harm my brother. He must take this food home to our family. They are starving … don't you understand?"

The huge bear let go of Pitohok's hand and the caribou's leg and stood there glaring back at her.

"Quick! Get back on your feet," Upik whispered. "We have only a little way to go."

The grizzly must have seen the snowhouse, too, for suddenly it shambled around in front of them, blocking Pitohok's way.

"I warned you not to hurt my brother!" Upik screamed again.

As if ruled by magic, the huge bear stepped back and let them pass.

"Mother! Mother! Come and help us!" Upik wailed.

Long Claws turned its head and stared at her when Upik's mother burst out of their igloo entrance. She saw the great humped shoulders of the akla and, like her daughter, screamed at it, then turned and rushed inside again.

Upik tried to take half of the caribou's weight on her own shoulders while pulling Pitohok to his feet. Slowly he rose, but his knees would scarcely support him.

"Don't drop it now," Upik said in a stern voice. "We're almost there."

Together they staggered painfully toward the igloo.

"Everything is whirling around," cried Pitohok. "It's going black again … I'm falling.…"

Because she no longer had the strength to hold him, Upik and her brother collapsed together on the snow. She shook him, but Pitohok seemed to have lost the power to hear or move or speak. Upik tried to drag him toward the igloo, but his arms remained locked tight around their precious burden of meat.

Long Claws turned once more and shambled after them, snarling like a huge and angry dog. It grasped the caribou's neck in its powerful jaws and started backing away, dragging the carcass and Pitohok, pulling both of them into the swirling fog.

The snow knife, the rifle, and Pitohok's short knife were gone. Upik had no weapons but her hands and teeth. She turned and saw her grandfather crawling out of the igloo on his hands and knees. In his left mitt he held his huge curved bow and in his mouth a pair of arrows. Right behind him came their mother, her parka hood puffed out with icy wind, screaming aloud, raging to protect her children, ready to do battle with the enormous bear. Her hands outstretched like claws, their mother raced forward to attack.

Upik heard her grandfather call out, "Stop, woman. Hold! If you help me, we can pierce him right from here."

The grandfather knelt unsteadily and notched an arrow to the braided string. His hands shook with strain when he tried to draw the powerful bow. But he could not. In desperation Upik's mother knelt and helped to draw the heavy weapon almost to full curve. The point of the arrow wavered wildly when the grandfather tried to aim.

"Don't!" Upik cried, spreading her arms and running between her grandfather's unsteady arrow and the bear. "You might hit Pitohok."

Looking back, she saw her brother still being dragged across the snow behind the bear. In sudden anger, she whirled around and ran straight between her brother and the akla, screaming, *"You let go of him! Let go!"*

Surprised, the huge grizzly released the caribou for a moment and raised its head.

"Here, this is for you," she yelled, and, reaching into her parka hood, she snatched out the last piece of frozen trout that she had saved and flung it beyond the bear.

The akla looked at her, grunted, then turned and moved away from Pitohok, who still clasped the caribou as fiercely as an Arctic crab. The grizzly snatched up the piece of fish. Then, with its hips and frosted shoulders rolling, it disappeared into the silver wall of icy fog.

Pitohok's mother and his grandfather knelt beside him, trying to unlock his arms from the caribou.

Pitohok opened his eyes and stared at them. "I thought that akla would surely snatch the caribou away from me," he whispered.

"I, too, believed that he would take it from you," his grandfather agreed. "But no human knows exactly what the animals will do."

"Upik was afraid of the akla. We were both afraid of him, and yet she ran and put her body between me and the grizzly's snarling jaws. Grandfather, did you believe my sister would do that?"

"No. I did not know what she would do. Nobody knows the strength or courage that humans possess until real danger comes to test them."

Reflect on

Strategies: How did thinking about the characteristics of suspense help you to enjoy this story? Find three examples of the characteristics of suspense to explain your answer.

Your Learning: Few children in Canada today have experiences like the brother and sister in this story. How are their lives in the Far North different from yours? How are they similar?

Biodiversity

In this unit, you will

- visualize while you read
- write concisely
- listen creatively
- identify characteristics of magazine covers and contents
- identify characteristics of descriptive text pattern
- learn about biodiversity

LET'S TALK

Animal Groups Quiz

1 Which of these animals belongs to the same group as the **Atlantic herring**?

Atlantic herring

garter snake

vulture

seal

catfish

2 Which of these animals belongs to the same group as the **flamingo**?

flamingo

Pacific salmon

bat

hummingbird

poison dart frog

Animals belong to different groups. The members of each group have certain characteristics in common. Take the quiz below to see if you can find the animals that belong to the same group.

3 Which of these animals belongs to the same group as the **chameleon**?

chameleon

parrot

turtle

giant armadillo

cane toad

4 Which of these animals belongs to the same group as the **lion**?

lion

beluga whale

crocodile

peregrine falcon

piranha

Understanding reading strategies

Visualizing

Visualizing helps you understand what an author is describing or explaining. You can use this strategy to draw mental pictures of familiar things or of things you have never seen before. You can also use visualizing to help you understand concepts.

Use comparisons to familiar things to help you understand concepts. Visualize the organization of your school library. Why is this classification system useful?

SCIENTIFIC Classification

by Todd Lo

bog copper butterfly

What Is Classification?

Classifying means organizing things into groups. The things in each group have something in common. For example, libraries use a classification system—usually numbers and letters—to organize books. Imagine trying to find a book in a library that didn't use a classification system! Scientists use a classification system to organize into groups the many different kinds of organisms (living things) found on Earth.

Just think of the variety of animals you've seen—everything from scaly, slithering snakes and snow-white polar bears to brightly coloured butterflies and razor-toothed sharks.

Plants are also living things and, like animals, they come in many different colours, shapes, and sizes—from towering trees to flowering garden plants and the many different crops that farmers grow.

There are even organisms that are not plants *or* animals, such as bacteria and mushrooms. Scientists have found ways to classify them, too.

How Does Scientific Classification Work?

Scientists divide all living things into groups called kingdoms. Then the kingdoms are divided into smaller groups, and those groups are divided into even smaller groups, and so on. As you move from larger to smaller groups, the organisms in each group have more in common.

Scientific Classification

Kingdoms: five groups that contain all living things

Phyla: each kingdom is divided into smaller groups called phyla (singular: phylum)

Classes: each phylum is divided into smaller groups called classes

Orders: each class is divided into smaller groups called orders

Families: each order is divided into smaller groups called families

Genera: each family is divided into smaller groups called genera (singular: genus)

Species: each genus is divided into smaller groups called species

Draw a visual organizer in your mind. What would you draw first in a visual organizer showing the classification of living things? What would you draw next?

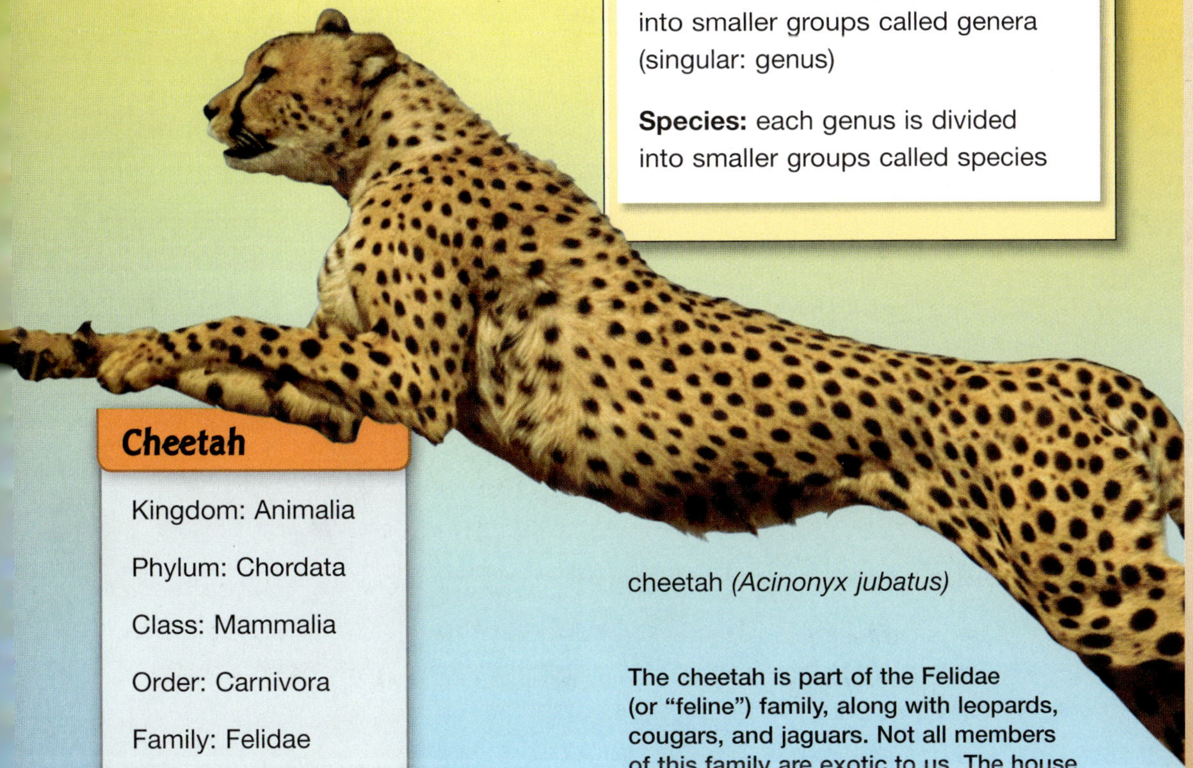

Cheetah

Kingdom: Animalia

Phylum: Chordata

Class: Mammalia

Order: Carnivora

Family: Felidae

Genus: *Acinonyx*

Species: *jubatus*

cheetah *(Acinonyx jubatus)*

The cheetah is part of the Felidae (or "feline") family, along with leopards, cougars, and jaguars. Not all members of this family are exotic to us. The house cat belongs to the same family.

Common and Scientific Names

We know many living things by their common names—the names people use to refer to them—such as badger. But each organism also has a scientific name made up of its genus and species names. Scientific names come from Latin.

European badger (*Meles meles*)

Why do organisms need scientific names? Because sometimes common names can be confusing. For example, the animal called a badger in Europe is not the same species that we call a badger in Canada, even though the two look quite similar. The scientific name for the European badger is *Meles meles*, and the badger found in Canada has the scientific name *Taxidea taxus*.

Canadian badger (*Taxidea taxus*)

Five of the Kingdoms

Moneran Kingdom

Monera are tiny, single-celled organisms. Unlike the cells of all other living things, a moneran does not have a nucleus (a dark mass at its centre). Bacteria and blue-green algae are examples of monera. There are over 3000 known species of monera.

Identify important information so you can draw accurate pictures in your mind. What words help you visualize the difference between a moneran and a protist?

Protist Kingdom

Protists are single-celled organisms. Protists have a nucleus and other cell parts called organelles. Protists live in water or in damp places. An amoeba is an example of a protist. There are more than 28 000 known species of protist.

Fungus Kingdom

Fungi are mostly multicellular organisms. They absorb food from other organisms, which may be dead or alive. Moulds, mushrooms, and mildew are examples of fungi. There are about 75 000 known species of fungus.

fly agaric mushroom

Use numbers to visualize quantity. Which kingdom has the most known species? Which has the least?

Plant Kingdom

Plants are multicellular organisms. The cells in a plant contain a green substance called chlorophyll. The cells use chlorophyll to make their own food from water and sunlight. There are more than 400 000 known species of plant.

rafflesia plant

Animal Kingdom

Animals are multicellular organisms. Their cells cannot make their own food, so most animals must move around to feed. There are over 1 300 000 known species of animal.

spider

Animals: Invertebrates and Vertebrates

by Rochelle Strauss

Applying Strategies

Visualizing

As you read, use visualizing to help you understand what you are reading:

- Use comparisons to familiar things to help you understand concepts.
- Draw a visual organizer in your mind.
- Identify important information so you can draw accurate pictures in your mind.
- Use numbers to visualize quantity.

Animals (1 318 000 Species)

From lions, tigers, and bears to jellyfish, sponges, and sea slugs, the animal kingdom is the largest and most diverse of the kingdoms.

The species in this kingdom are further grouped into invertebrates (animals without backbones, such as spiders, insects, sponges, and worms) and vertebrates (animals with backbones—fish, birds, reptiles, amphibians, and mammals).

With or without backbones, all animals share some characteristics. Unlike plants, animals cannot create their own food. They rely on other life forms for food. Some animals (herbivores) eat plants, while others (carnivores) eat the animals that eat the plants. Some animals (omnivores) eat both plants and animals.

Plants rely on animals, too. Most flowering plants need animals, especially insects, to take pollen from one flower to another so that new seeds can form. Without animals, many plants could not produce seeds.

Animals also help spread plant seeds. Birds and bats eat the fruit the plants produce. The fruit is digested and the seeds are dropped in the animal's waste, away from the adult plant. This gives the new plants room to grow.

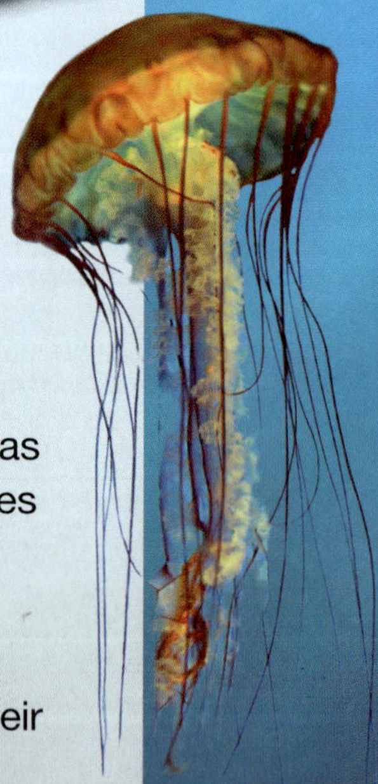

jellyfish

bee

giant squid

Invertebrates (1 265 500 Species)

Invertebrates live everywhere on Earth—on land and in water. They range from sea sponges, corals, and jellyfish to insects, spiders, and worms. About the only thing they all have in common is that none of them have a backbone. Instead, many have an exoskeleton—a tough, outer covering that protects them.

Of all the invertebrates, insects are probably the most familiar, for good reason—they make up more than three-quarters of all invertebrates.

Some invertebrates are enormous. The giant squid is probably the biggest invertebrate on Earth. It can grow up to 18 m long and weigh over 450 kg. Even its eyes are huge—as big as basketballs.

But most invertebrates are small enough that you'd easily overlook them. Their size makes them so difficult to find that scientists believe there may be millions more invertebrates still to be discovered and named.

Some Types of Invertebrates

75 000 arachnids
(e.g., spiders, ticks, mites, horseshoe crabs)

70 000 mollusks
(e.g., snails, sea slugs, mussels, octopuses, squid)

40 000 crustaceans
(e.g., lobsters, crabs, crayfish, shrimp, barnacles)

9000 cnidarians
(e.g., jellyfish, corals, sea anemones)

Vertebrates (52 500 Species)

Vertebrates are the animals we know best. Why? Because even without a microscope, they are easy to find. All it takes is a quick look in a mirror to bring you face to face with one. But although vertebrates are all around us, they make up only a tiny portion of the species on Earth.

Vertebrates are subdivided into fish, birds, reptiles, amphibians, and mammals. The main thing they have in common is a backbone, which is made up of a series of bones called vertebrae. The vertebrae house and protect the spinal cord, which works with the brain to control everything in the body. Vertebrates also have an internal skeleton that allows for movement, support, and protection.

Today, vertebrates can be found on land and in water. But the first vertebrates lived only in the seas. About 360 million years ago, some of these creatures started to move out of the sea, and vertebrate life on land began.

cardinal

Types of Vertebrates
25 100 fish
9800 birds
8000 reptiles
4960 amphibians
4640 mammals

wildebeest

Reflect on

Strategies: Find a place where you drew a visual organizer in your mind to help you understand what you were reading.

Your Learning: Which group in the animal kingdom is most interesting to you? What would you like to find out about this group?

Understanding writing strategies

Planning for Concise Writing

Concise writing communicates a strong message with a few well-chosen words.

Gwendolyn wanted to tell her classmates about her pet tortoise. She used a web to brainstorm main ideas and precise, descriptive words and phrases.

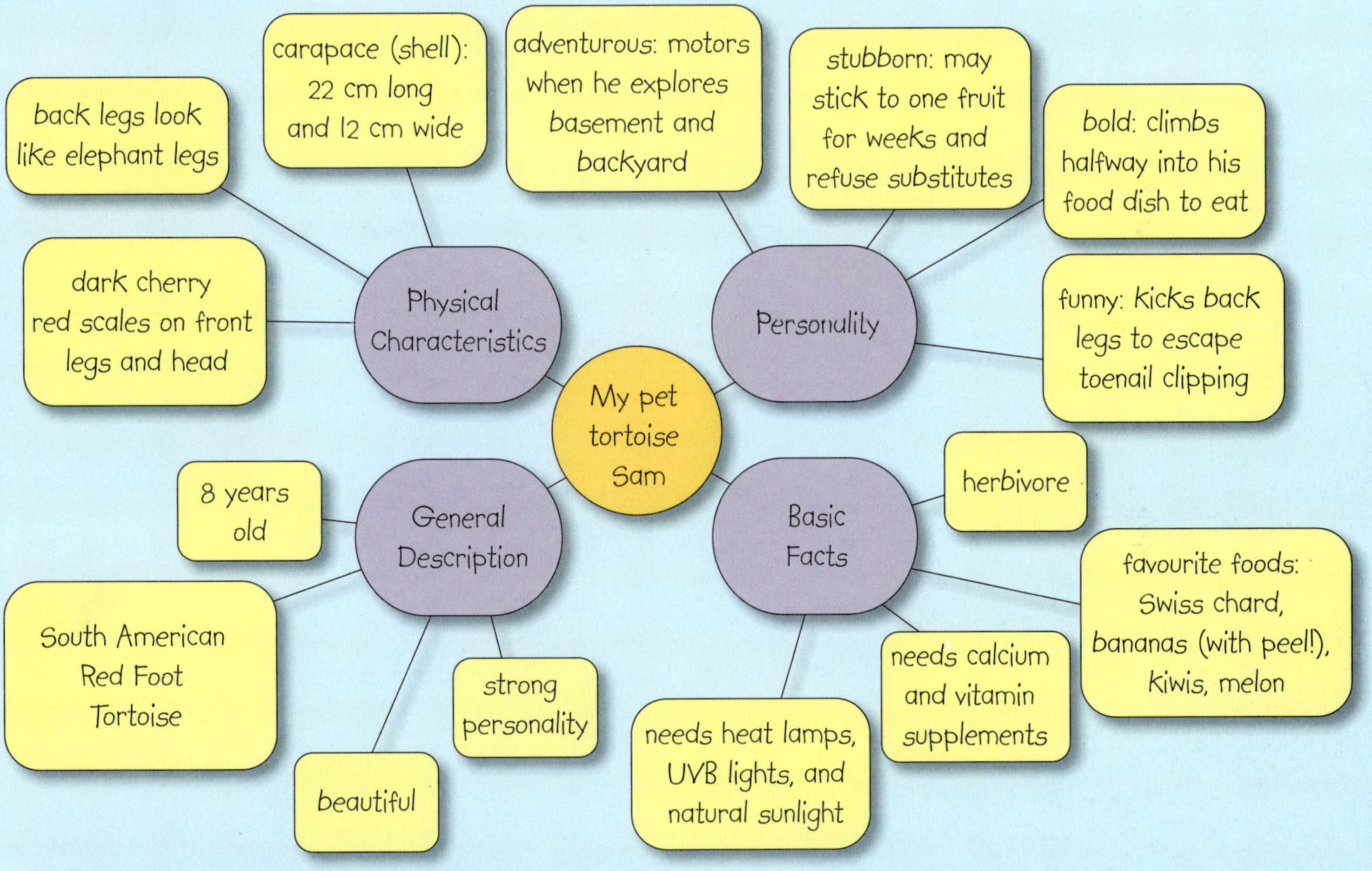

How to make writing concise:

- ✔ Think about your message and main ideas.
- ✔ Use a web or other graphic organizer to brainstorm ideas.
- ✔ Write down precise words and descriptive phrases.

BLOND, FURRY,

Applying Strategies

Reading Like a Writer

As you read, notice how the author made her writing concise. Identify precise words and descriptive phrases. Look for places where the writer communicates a strong idea with just a few words.

by Barbara Hehner

More than 2000 m below the surface of the Pacific Ocean, the water is inky black. But the bright headlights of a submersible—a small undersea exploring vehicle—picked out odd little creatures scuttling across the ocean floor. They were about 15 cm long and moved like crabs on 10 legs. The French and American scientists in the submersible knew at once that these animals were something they had never seen before. For one thing, their legs were covered in long, thick, blond hair!

Yeti crab

AND DEEP IN THE OCEAN

A new species is a thrilling discovery for any researcher. But the animal discovered by the scientific team was even rarer and stranger than that. The "Yeti crab" was so different from its closest relatives, crabs, that it needed a new family and genus as well. The team decided to name the crab *Kiwa*, after a Polynesian guardian of the ocean. This became the genus name. They used the Latin word *hirsuta*, which means "hairy," as the species name. The family name became Kiwaidae. The crab was given the common name "Yeti" after the legendary furry creature that is said to live in the Himalayas.

There is a lot still to learn about *Kiwa hirsuta*. Is it blind? The scientists noted that its eyes were tiny and had no pigment (colouring). The animal probably does not need vision in the dark depths of the ocean. Is *Kiwa hirsuta* a carnivore? Scientists think it might be, because they saw it fighting with two crabs over a piece of shrimp.

There is one thing scientists have determined for certain—the *Kiwa hirsuta* that they brought to the surface for study smelled terrible. It lives beside gassy vents in the ocean floor that smell like rotten eggs, and it picks up the odour. They also discovered that the long, blond hairs are full of bacteria. Why is this so? Scientists have two theories: The bacteria may be part of *Kiwa hirsuta's* diet, or they may filter poisons from the vents that would otherwise harm the creature.

Yeti Crab

Kingdom: Animalia

Phylum: Arthropoda

Class: Malacostraca

Order: Decapoda

Family: Kiwaidae

Genus: *Kiwa*

Species: *hirsuta*

Reflect on

Writer's Craft: Find a place in the article where concise writing helped you visualize something that was not shown in the photograph.

Your Learning: What did you learn about the jobs of the research scientists who discovered the Yeti crab?

Understanding media

Staying in Touch with Nature

Identifying Characteristics of Magazine Covers and Contents

Magazines give readers up-to-date information on a vast number of topics. Often, you will find several different magazines on a popular topic. How can you decide which one to read? Knowing the characteristics of magazine covers and Contents will help you make good choices.

The cover gives information about the magazine. Find the name and date of this magazine.

The cover grabs readers' attention with a striking image and gives highlights of what's inside. What draws your attention to this magazine? Which article would you look inside to find?

CANADIAN Geographic

MAKING CANADA BETTER KNOWN TO CANADIANS AND TO THE WORLD

FEATURES

PICTORIAL AND POSTER

NATURE'S CRADLE 36
Salty marshes, boreal bogs and soggy swamps: wetlands are the planet's watery nurseries of life
By Dane Lanken and Elizabeth Shilts

WILDLIFE

OWL INFLUX 44
Alberta hosts a rare bird reunion
By Wayne Lynch

RESOURCES

WATER WORKS 50
Freshwater supplies are drying up in many countries, but Canadians still treat water like an unlimited resource
By Marq de Villiers

RESTORATION

GREEN CITY 60
How 30 years of grassroots determination is erasing Sudbury's industrial gloom
By David Lees with photography by Mike Grandmaison

SCIENCE

ON THE LOOKOUT 72
Quebec's Mont-Saint-Hilaire becomes a sentinel in a nationwide environmental early-warning network
By Ian Austen with photography by Francis Lépine

Wet worlds, p. 36

Great grey rendezvous, p. 44

Taking root, p. 60

A red-throated loon nests in a wetland near Igloolik, Nunavut.

May/June 2000, Vol. 120, No. 4

The Contents lists articles and provides page numbers like a Contents in a book. Often, the Contents tells a bit about each article. What does this Contents page tell about the article "Water Works"?

The Contents often shows how a magazine is organized. What kinds of articles are listed in the Features section?

Imagine you are standing at a magazine rack in a library or a store. You're looking for a magazine about the natural world. What can you learn about this magazine by previewing the cover and Contents? Which magazine would you choose, this one or the one on the previous page?

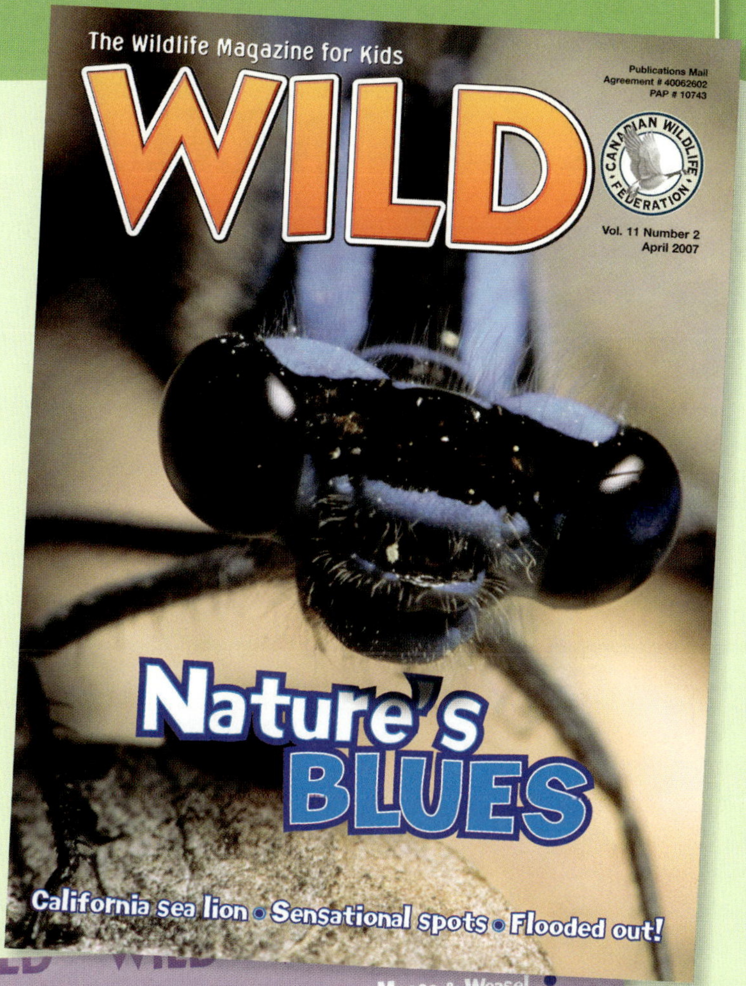
The Wildlife Magazine for Kids

WILD

Publications Mail
Agreement # 40062602
PAP # 10743

CANADIAN WILDLIFE FEDERATION

Vol. 11 Number 2
April 2007

Nature's BLUES

California sea lion • Sensational spots • Flooded out!

INSIDE WILD
April 2007
Vol. 11 No. 2

Front cover: Bluet damselfly (Wayne Lynch)
Back cover: Red fox (Wayne Lynch)

2

3

Understanding text patterns

Identifying Characteristics of Descriptive Text Pattern

Writers often use descriptive text pattern to describe the attributes of one thing. Descriptive text pattern has certain characteristics:

- The topic is clearly identified.
- The attributes of the topic are presented in sections.
- Each section answers questions such as "What is it?" "What does it look like?" and "What is its purpose?"
- Details describe something important about the topic using sensory language.

MARVELLOUS MOUTHS

by Pamela Hickman

The mouth is the first stop that food makes on its way through an animal's body. Mouths come in many shapes and sizes, and most mouths are adapted to the kind of food that an animal eats. Some insect eaters have extra-long tongues for catching and pulling in their prey. A snake's special jaws can open wide enough to swallow food that is larger than the snake's own head.

← The topic is clearly identified. What is the topic of this article?

Meat-Eating Teeth

Carnivores are well equipped with sharp teeth for killing and tearing up their food. The crocodile has large, strong jaws and cone-shaped teeth for grabbing prey and dragging it underwater. In its lifetime, a crocodile can grow up to 3000 teeth!

Crocodiles have strong stomach juices to help digest food, including bones, hooves, and antlers.

The crocodile has another adaptation that comes in handy when it drags prey underwater. In its throat there is a flap that keeps water out when the crocodile dives with a big meal in its mouth.

↗ The attributes of the topic are presented in sections. What attribute of mouths does this section describe?

Blue whales weigh more than 2 t when born and can grow to be longer than a basketball court.

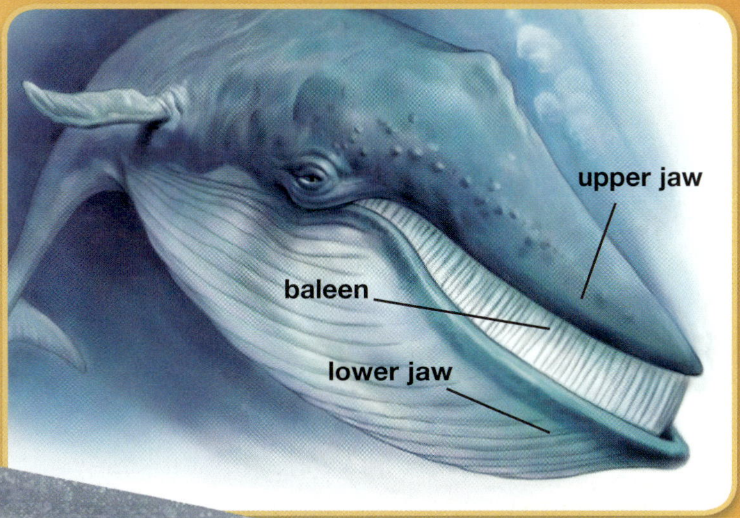

Baleen Banquet

Animals have different kinds of teeth adapted to the food they eat. Instead of having teeth, the blue whale has stiff, black plates called baleen hanging from the roof of its mouth. When the whale feeds, it opens up its mouth and sucks in ocean water containing tiny animals. The whale then closes its mouth and raises its enormous tongue to force the water back out through the baleen. The baleen works like a sieve, trapping food inside the whale's mouth. The whale's tongue scrapes the baleen clean and the animal swallows the food.

Each day, an adult blue whale eats 5–7 t of krill, a tiny shrimp-like creature. Baby blue whales drink more than 200 L of their mother's milk per day—and can gain 90 kg a day!

Each section answers questions such as "What does it look like?" What does the mouth of the blue whale look like?

←

←

Each section has details that describe something important about the topic using sensory language. How does the whale's baleen mouth work?

The vampire bat has special sensors on its nose. These sensors help the bat to locate the best place to bite its prey—an area where blood flows close to the skin.

A Liquid Diet

For some animals, drinking is not just a way of getting water, it is also how they get their food. When a spider catches a fly in its web, the spider doesn't actually eat the fly. Instead, it drinks the fluids from the fly's body. Vampire bats are famous for their diet of blood. Using its tiny, sharp teeth, a vampire bat makes a small cut in a mammal's or a bird's skin and laps up the flowing blood with its tongue.

Each section answers questions such as "What is its purpose?" What purpose do liquids have for some animals?

The lamprey is well adapted for its role of feeding on the blood of other fish. Instead of jaws, the lamprey has a round, sucking mouth that clings to its prey. Inside the mouth are as many as 125 sharp teeth. The lamprey works its teeth back and forth to drill a hole into the prey's body. Glands inside the mouth produce a liquid that keeps the prey's blood flowing. Lampreys don't kill their prey on the first attack, but weaken them. Fish often die later, after several lamprey attacks.

Each section has details that describe something important about the topic using sensory language. How does the lamprey use its mouth to get food?

Lampreys have circular mouths with many rows of teeth.

COYOTES THE SUPER ADAPTERS

by Diane Swanson

When animals are forced to seek out new habitats, they may find themselves living in conditions quite different from the ones they're used to. Survival often depends on their ability to adapt to new surroundings.

Applying Strategies

Identifying Characteristics of Descriptive Text Pattern

As you read, identify characteristics of descriptive text pattern:

- The topic is clearly identified.
- The attributes of the topic are presented in sections.
- Each section answers questions such as "What is it?" "What does it look like?" and "What is its purpose?"
- Details describe something important about the topic using sensory language.

Home, Sweet Home

Bigger than a fox but smaller than a wolf, the bushy-tailed coyote is the most adaptable dog in North America—the only place on Earth that it lives. If you change the food supply, the coyote changes what it eats. Build a city and the coyote moves right in.

Today, most wild animals live in fewer regions than they once did, but coyotes live in even more. As cities grew, the number of forests decreased. This left fewer places for the wolf, the coyote's main enemy, to find a home. With less competition, the coyote could spread out and occupy more land. In Canada, coyotes lived on the Prairies and in Southern British Columbia in the early 1800s. A hundred years later, they were also in Ontario, Québec, and the Northern territories. By the 1960s, they had reached the East Coast.

When coyotes settle into a new area, they can triple their population there within a year. As individuals, they also do well—even in back alleys, empty lots, and golf courses of big cities. In fact, city coyotes often grow larger than country coyotes because city eating is so good.

Chow Time

It's easy for coyotes to feed in the city. They are not fussy eaters. Coyotes steal food, like watermelons and cantaloupes, from crates behind stores. They raid gardens, digging under—or climbing over—tall fences to get seeds, vegetables, and fruit. They even pick through leftovers in neighbourhood garbage cans, or eat dead animals.

Midnight Snack at the Golf Course

You might not head to the golf course when you get hungry, but coyotes in Vancouver, British Columbia, often do. It's a choice spot for hunting mice and squirrels. And at night, coyotes have the place to themselves.

Another favourite place is the city's huge Stanley Park, home to many squirrels and rabbits. Coyotes travel along a beach to get to the park, coming and going in the early morning and evening.

Coyotes also hunt most of the other animals that live in cities, including mice, rats, squirrels, small dogs, cats, rabbits, skunks, raccoons, birds, snakes, lizards, fish, frogs, turtles—even insects. Coyotes depend mostly on a keen sense of smell to sniff out prey. They also use their sharp ears to hear small animals that creep through the grass. Keeping their slim bodies near the ground, coyotes sneak up on their prey, then pounce. They can leap a distance more than twice the length of a bed.

If they have to chase their prey, coyotes can run 40 km/h and, in short bursts, 65 km/h. Besides being swift runners, they twist and turn quickly, using their long tails for balance. Although coyotes usually hunt alone, one may chase an animal, like a rabbit, toward another coyote hiding under a bush.

Coyotes swim well and may dive into ponds or streams to catch prey such as crayfish. They also stick their heads underwater to nab fish with their teeth.

Coyote

Kingdom: Animalia

Phylum: Chordata

Class: Mammalia

Order: Carnivora

Family: Canidae

Genus: *Canis*

Species: *latrans*

Reflect on

Strategies: What attributes of coyotes did the writer present? How does listing the attributes help you think about what you have learned?

Critical Literacy: Think about the title of the article. What do you think is the writer's point of view on coyotes? What other points of view on coyotes might the writer have left out?

Understanding **listening** strategies

Creative Listening

You have experience listening for facts. You listen for facts when a classmate is giving a report, or when you are watching a science movie. Creative listening is a way to take the facts and turn them into a new understanding of a topic.

Watch as this student practises creative listening to build a new understanding.

How to listen creatively:

- ☑ Connect facts to your personal experience.
- ☑ Ask yourself questions.
- ☑ Use visualizing to help you pull ideas together in new ways.

The Polar Bear

by Victoria Miles

Dr. Ian Stirling, a senior research scientist for the Canadian Wildlife Service, is considered to be a world expert on polar bears. While studying the polar bears on Devon Island, Nunavut, he observed some fighting behaviour he'd never seen before.

Putting It All Together

As you read, remember to use the strategies you learned in this unit:

- Visualize to help you understand what you are reading.
- Recognize concise writing.
- Identify characteristics of descriptive text pattern.

Polar bears typically mate in April and May.

From the Field

Ian had his telescope focused on a "very, very large male" with a female in his company. As Ian watched, a challenger male with long, black scars came into sight. Under its white coat, a polar bear's skin is black. When a bear is wounded, the cut heals over, but fur does not grow back over the scar. This newcomer was obviously an experienced fighter and a battle over the female was about to break out on the ice.

Male polar bears often fight each other for mating rights.

These polar-bear images show various fighting stances.

Ian had seen bears fight for mating rights plenty of times before. He knew that the scraps could last well over a half hour, so he settled down to watch the fight unfold.

But the big, dominant male had a surprise in store. He took a lunging rush at the intruder, grabbed his neck in his jaws, flipped him over, and pinned him to the ice. He stood there, his teeth wrapped around the throat of his challenger, for 10 or 20 seconds. "He took just enough time to show who was boss, then he let him go," says Ian. A couple of days later a second bear, as scarred with experience as the first, "got thumped just as quickly." Ian had never seen such a fast fight. "Clearly," he says, "this dominant male was at the top of the heap."

Animal Notes

Size and Weight

Full-grown male polar bears typically weigh between 350 and 650 kg. Adult females are between 150 and 250 kg, although a pregnant female may be as large as 500 kg. Polar bear cubs weigh about 0.6 kg at birth. In their first two years (if they survive), they will grow to be almost as big as their mothers.

Description

The polar bear has white fur, while its nose, lips, and eyes are black. A polar bear's skin under the fur is also black. Its thick fur, tough skin, and a blubber layer keep it warm.

Reproduction

April and May are the mating months for polar bears. Males challenge each other for mating rights with females. Litters of one to four cubs are usually born between November and January in a winter den. On average, a female has a litter only every three years. The cubs remain with their mother for about a year and a half, denning with her the winter after their birth. Still, only about 6 out of every 10 cubs make it through the first year of life. The others are killed by starvation, attacks by male polar bears, and accidents.

Food

The polar bear is the most carnivorous bear in North America. Seals are its main food. A polar bear will wait at a seal's breathing hole in the ice without moving, often for hours. Polar bears also eat fish, birds, birds' eggs, small mammals, and dead animals. Fat is so important to a polar bear's diet that it will not spend its own energy to eat a scrawny seal pup. A successful polar bear may eat every three or four days, but if food is scarce it might go two weeks between meals.

Lifespan

Male polar bears commonly live to be about 25 years of age. Females often live into their late 20s.

Habitat

Polar bears are found throughout the ice-covered waters of the Arctic region and prefer to remain on the sea ice all year if possible. As the ice retreats north during the summer months, polar bears travel with the ice floes.

Range

Polar bears are usually found in the northern marine areas of the state of Alaska, Norway's Svalbard Archipelago, Russia, Greenland, and Canada.

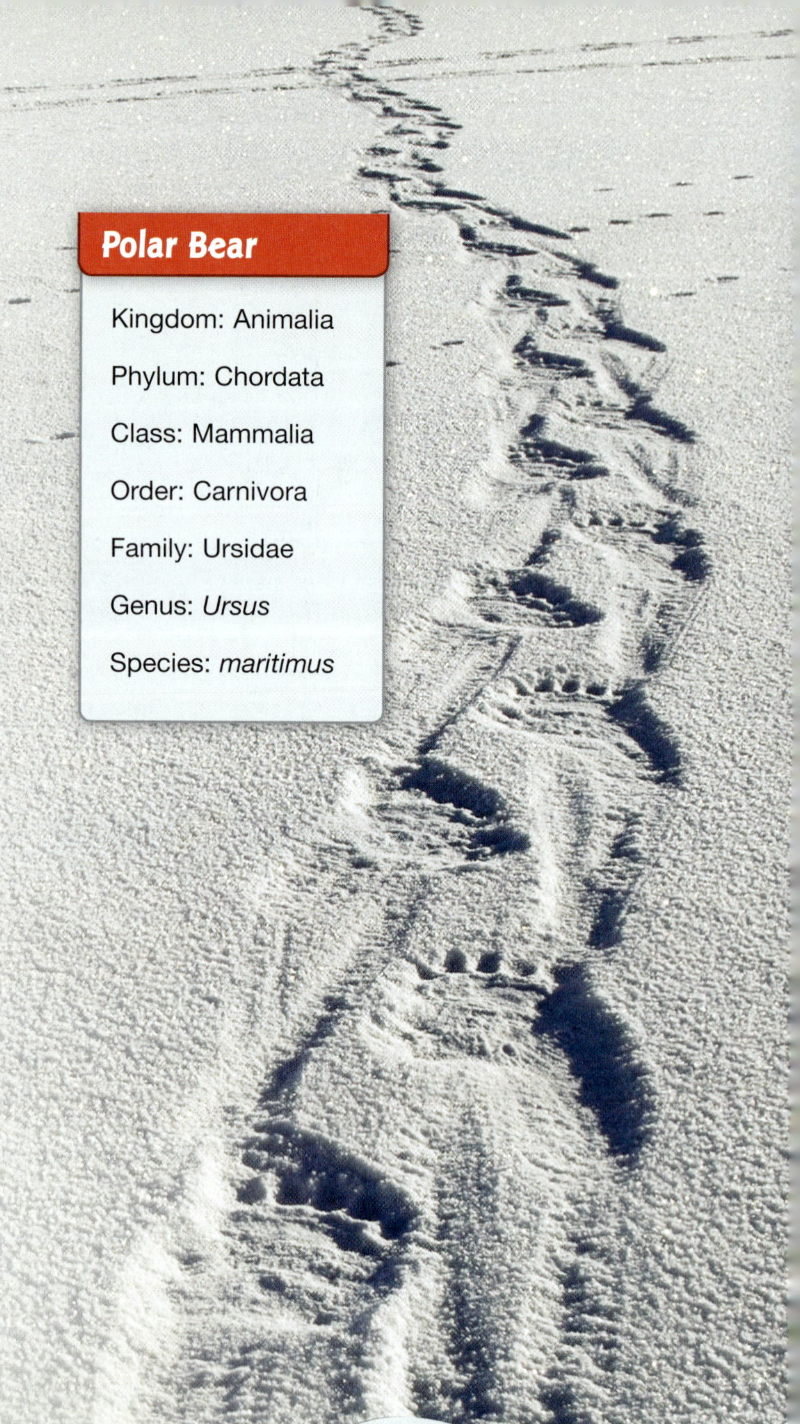

Polar Bear

Kingdom: Animalia

Phylum: Chordata

Class: Mammalia

Order: Carnivora

Family: Ursidae

Genus: *Ursus*

Species: *maritimus*

Reflect on

Strategies: How did visualizing help you understand something new about polar bears? What attributes of polar bears did you learn about?

Connections: Think about books, TV shows, or movies where you have seen polar bears before. How did your prior knowledge help you make connections to this article?

Social Studies

First Nations and Early Explorers

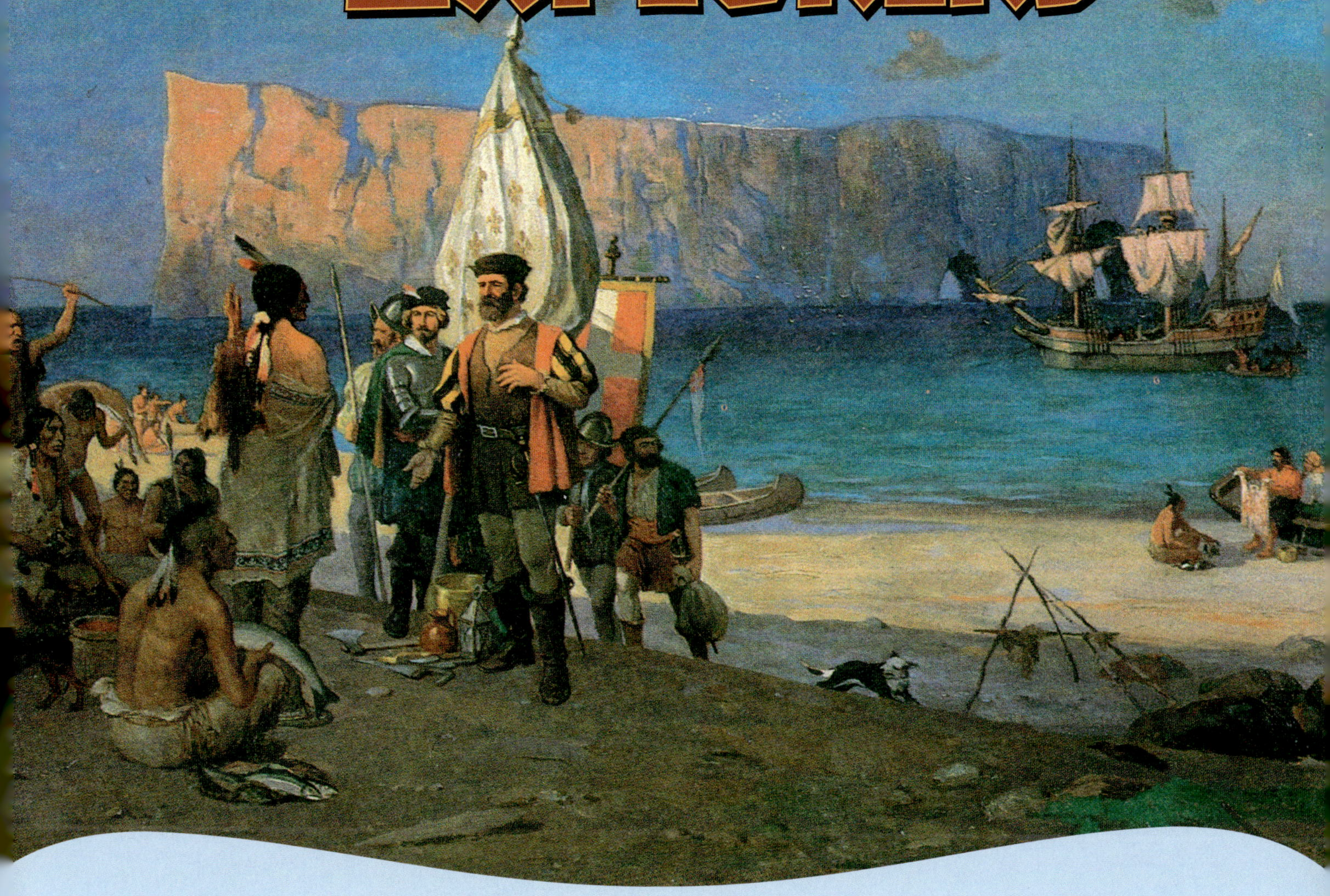

In this unit, you will

- predict using text features
- use visuals to understand text
- identify strong transitions
- identify conventions and techniques in art
- learn about First Peoples and European explorers

LET'S TALK

Ask the Artists

"No two tipis are ever pitched the same"
Gerald McMaster

"Enfolding"
Daphne Odjig

Canadian Museum of Civilization
Douglas Cardinal, architect

Take a look at these recent artistic works by Aboriginal people in Canada. What questions would you want to ask each person about his or her work?

"Flight"
Susan Point

"Elders Only"
Nance Ackerman

"Red Bull Moose"
Alan Syliboy

understanding reading strategies

Predicting

When you predict, you make guesses about what will happen next or what you will learn. Text features can help you make predictions before and during reading.

Read the introductory text. How does the introduction stand out from the rest of the text? What do you predict you will learn by reading this article?

Use visuals to help you predict what the text will be about. What text features accompany this map? What can you predict about the article by studying the map?

The First Peoples

Adapted from text by Ron Munro

The First Nations and Inuit are called the First Peoples because they are the original inhabitants of North America. While the seven groups who made up the First Peoples in Canada shared many beliefs, their traditional ways of life were quite different.

Major groups of First Peoples

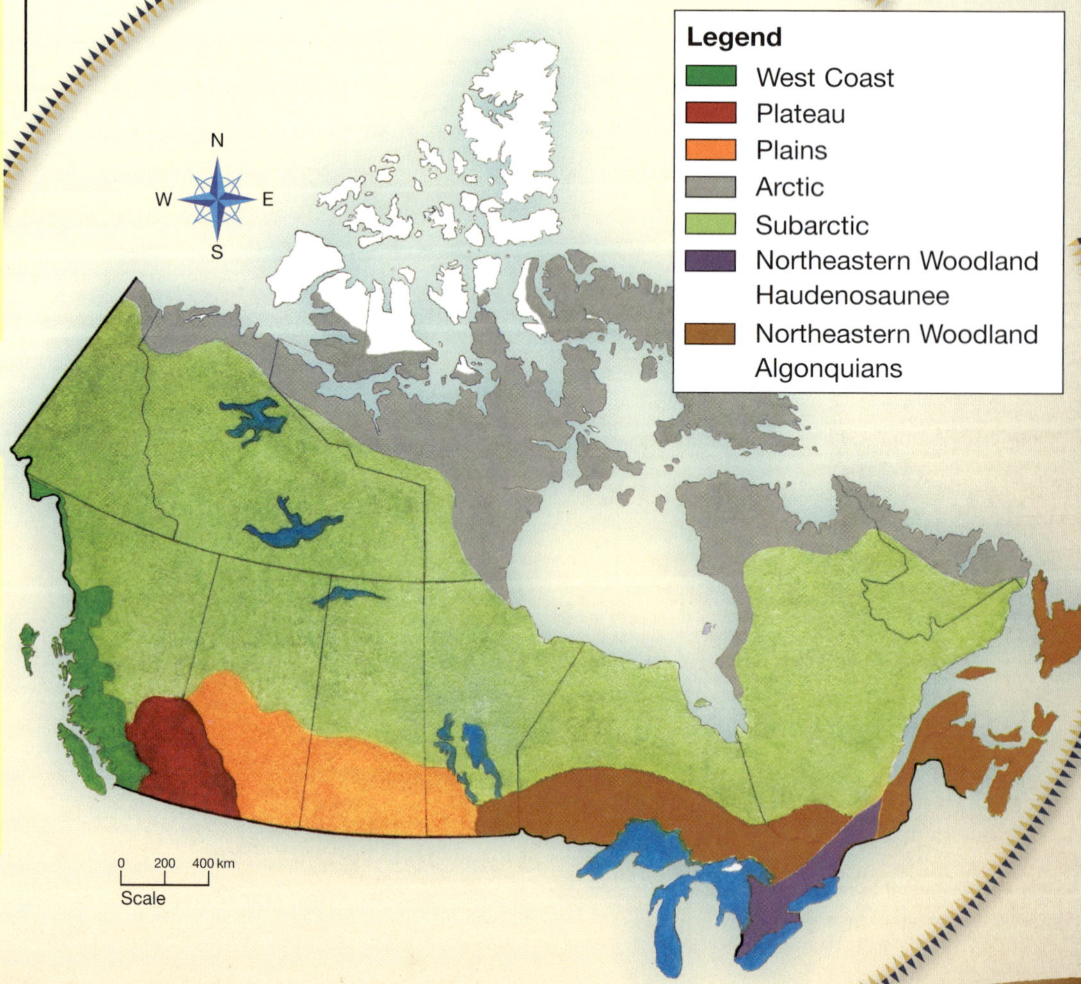

# of Canada

The First Peoples used materials nature provided to make clothing, shelters, tools and forms of transportation, such as this cedar canoe.

Shared Beliefs

Many different groups of First Peoples lived, and continue to live, across the land we now call Canada. All of these groups believed that land could not be owned. The land and its resources, such as wood, fish, and game, were shared among all the people.

The First Peoples also believed in living in harmony with nature. This means that they used resources wisely, never taking more than they needed. In this way, they saved resources for future generations.

Different Ways of Life

First Peoples lived off the land in different ways. In Canada's northeastern forests, the people hunted game and caught fish. In the warmer Great Lakes region, the First Peoples grew crops, such as corn and squash.

On the prairies, the people relied almost entirely on the buffalo. Along the west coast, people ate salmon and used the rainforest trees to build homes and canoes. On the tundra and in the Far North, caribou and seals were important animals people relied on to survive.

Tents made from animal skin were one form of shelter made by Inuit.

Use visuals to help you predict what the text will be about. What can you predict by looking at these photographs? Read to check your predictions.

Let's take a closer look at how these various groups of First Peoples lived off the land.

Fishers and Farmers of the Northeastern Woodlands

Preview the title and headings. How can you identify the main heading and the subheading on this page? What can you predict?

The Northeastern Woodlands stretch from the eastern coast to the west of Lake Superior. Two different groups lived in this region.

Coastal Fishers and Hunters

The First Peoples along the Atlantic Coast lived in a land that was rich with resources. The forests and oceans that surrounded them provided many different sources of food.

The people lived according to the seasons. As spring approached, they settled in villages along the coast. In summer, the ocean provided plenty of food, including shellfish, seals, and walruses. The people made canoes from birch bark sealed with sticky spruce gum. Using the rivers, they canoed inland where they hunted game and gathered fruits and nuts.

In autumn, they moved inland for the winter. They hunted moose, deer, bears, and otters. The meat was preserved and stored for winter. At their winter villages, they covered their homes with fur skins for added warmth.

Mi'kmaq were coastal fishers and hunters who used coloured quills to decorate small containers.

The soil was fertile and the climate mild where the Haudenosaunee people lived. They were able to grow most of their food in fields around their villages.

People of the Longhouse

The Haudenosaunee (Iroquois) were a group of five different First Nations who lived around the Great Lakes in what is now Southern Ontario. The fertile soil and mild climate of this region made farming possible. They grew corn, beans, squash, potatoes, turnips, and tomatoes. Because the Haudenosaunee relied on farming for food, they stayed in one place.

The crop fields surrounded each village, which was protected by a log stockade. Within the village were clusters of large homes called longhouses. Ten or more families lived together in each longhouse.

Hunters of the Great Plains

The Great Plains cover a vast area across the centre of North America. In the eastern section, tall prairie grasslands once covered the flat landscape. There were few trees on the plains, and few rivers, too.

The people of the Great Plains followed the herds of buffalo that roamed the prairies. The buffalo provided food and materials to make clothing, shelter, and tools. Tipis were made of long poles covered by buffalo skins.

As many as 60 million buffalo once roamed the prairies.

Use visuals to help you predict what the text will be about. What can you predict by looking at the painting and photos on these two pages?

Use visuals to help you predict what the text will be about. What can you predict by looking at the photos on these two pages

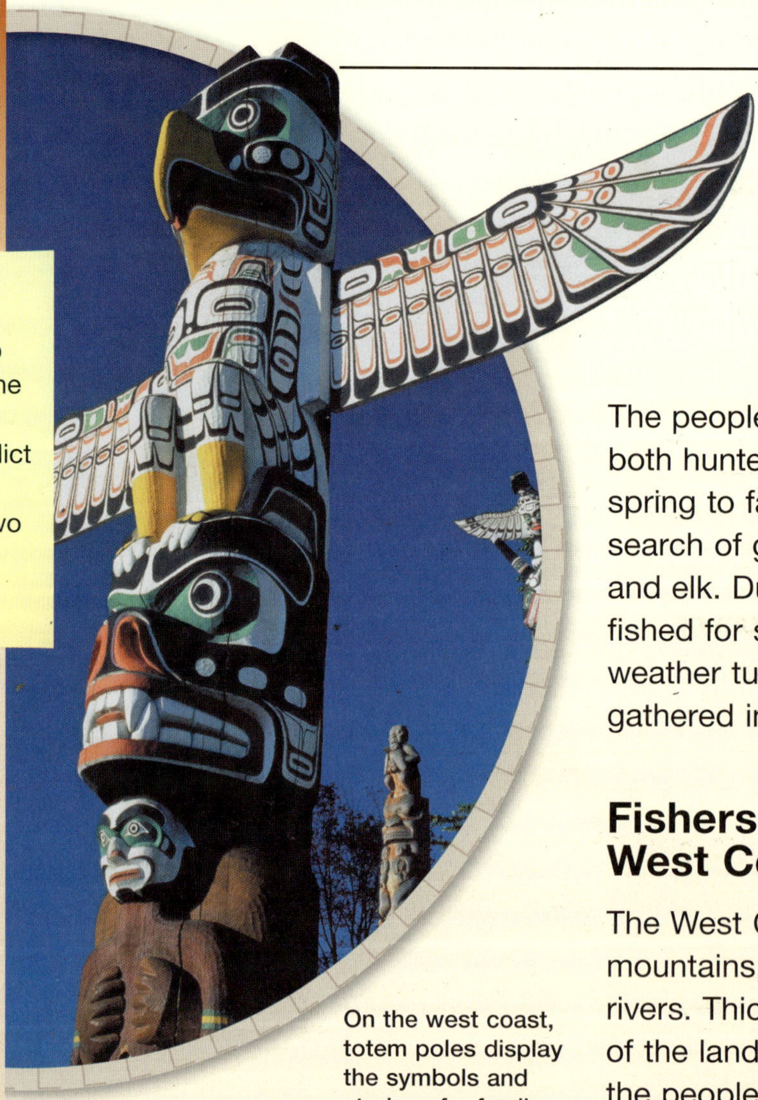

On the west coast, totem poles display the symbols and stories of a family or clan (group of related families).

Peoples of the Western Plateau

The Western Plateau covers land in southwestern Alberta and southeastern British Columbia. In the northern areas there are high mountains, thick forests, and lakes. Land in the south is covered by desert.

The people of the Plateau were both hunters and fishers. From spring to fall, they travelled in search of game such as deer and elk. During summer, they fished for salmon. When the weather turned cold, people gathered in winter villages.

Fishers of the West Coast

The West Coast is a land of mountains, islands, lakes, and rivers. Thick forests cover much of the land. Along the shores, the people fished and gathered shellfish. From the rainforests came the cedar logs they used to build their homes and canoes. Using fibres from the cedar bark, people wove clothing and blankets.

Since food was so easily available, the people of the West Coast had time to create many artistic works, such as colourful totem poles and masks.

Hunters on the Tundra

The Subarctic is an enormous region. There are thick forests in the south, then only small trees and shrubs farther north. In the most northern areas, there is open tundra—flat, treeless land.

Many different cultures lived in the Subarctic region. Their survival depended on hunting moose, bear, and caribou. Caribou meat was the main food source, and all parts of the animal were used to make such things as clothing, tents, snowshoes, and tools.

Inuit of the Far North

Inuit adapted very successfully to life in the Arctic. In summer, they travelled to hunt game such as caribou, muskoxen, bears, and waterfowl. On the coast, they gathered shellfish and berries, caught fish, and hunted marine animals. Inuit moved frequently, returning to their favourite places each year.

Inuit created many unique inventions to help them survive. These include the iglu and the kayak—a slender, lightweight boat used for hunting.

Inuit used kayaks to hunt marine animals and sea birds.

First Nations and

Adapted from text by
Dr. Cornelius J. Jaenen

Applying Strategies

Predicting

As you read, make predictions to help you understand what you are reading. Use text features to help you make predictions.

- Preview the title and headings.
- Read the introduction to help you predict what the text will be about.
- Use visuals to help you predict what the text will be about.

From time immemorial, the First Nations had been the only inhabitants of North America. But that changed when European explorers began crossing the Atlantic Ocean.

Why did Europeans come to North America? They were searching for a faster route to China, Japan, and India. They did not find this route, but they did find a land that was rich in natural resources, and they made contact with the peoples who lived here.

New Trade Route from Europe to Asia

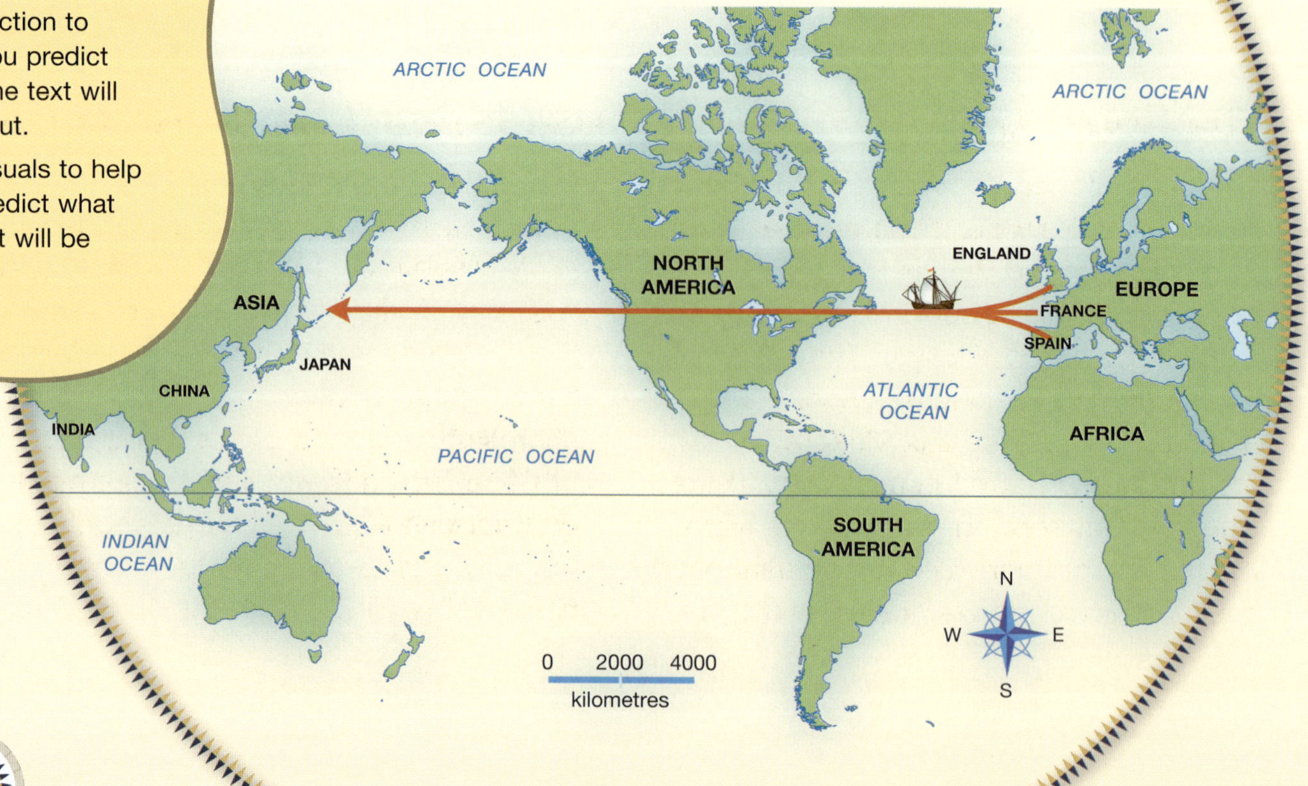

Europeans sailed west in search of Asia and found North America.

First Contacts

The first tall Viking ships must have been a startling sight to the Beothuks.

The Norse Arrive

The Beothuk people lived in the region that we now call Newfoundland and Labrador. Sometime around the year 1100, strangers appeared on their shores. These were the Norse (also called Vikings). They had sailed across from Greenland and soon built a settlement at L'Anse aux Meadows. At first the Norse traded peacefully with the Beothuk, but soon the two groups were battling each other. The Norse abandoned their settlement and left Newfoundland.

Cabot Lands on North America

In 1497, the Italian-born explorer John Cabot (Giovanni Caboto) landed somewhere on the North American coast. The English king had sent him to explore the land on the other side of the Atlantic. It's not clear whether Cabot reached the shores of Newfoundland and Labrador, or Cape Breton Island. He did not make contact with the First Nations people of the area, but he did claim their land in the name of the King of England.

When he returned to England, Cabot reported that there were so many fish, they could be caught by simply lowering a bucket into the water. He returned to North America the following year, but his ship was lost and he was never heard from again.

Fishers from Europe were soon travelling to the area. They did make contact with the First Nations people and traded with them, exchanging European goods for furs.

Cartier Explores Eastern Canada

In 1534, French explorer Jacques Cartier set out to find a water route across North America to the Pacific Ocean. This would be a faster way for trading ships to reach Asia. On this first voyage, Cartier explored the Gulf of St. Lawrence. During his travels, he made contact with two First Nations groups, the Mi'kmaq and the Haudenosaunee (Iroquois). Both these groups traded their furs for European knives and iron goods.

Cartier realized that the land was rich in natural resources. He put up a large cross to claim the land for France. The Haudenosaunee chief, Donnacona, realized what Cartier was doing and became angry. Cartier convinced him that the cross was just a marker to help him find his way.

In 1497, John Cabot planted the English flag in North America and claimed the land for England.

Cartier Returns

Cartier took two of Chief Donnacona's sons back to France with him. When the French king heard their stories about the riches of Canada, he allowed Cartier to return the next year.

In 1535, Cartier sailed up the St. Lawrence River to Stadacona (now Québec City). Donnacona was the chief of this village of 500 people. Continuing along the St. Lawrence, Cartier reached a larger village called Hochelaga (now Montréal).

The next spring, Cartier forced Donnacona and nine others to return to France with him. Nine of the Haudenosaunee, including Donnacona, died while they were in France.

Champlain Brings French Settlers

Like Cartier, the French explorer Samuel de Champlain hoped to find a passage to Asia. In 1603 he sailed to North America and travelled up the St. Lawrence River. When he did not find a route to Asia, he returned to France.

Champlain returned the following year with 80 French settlers, and they spent the winter on a small island named Ste. Croix. The settlers were not prepared for the harsh winter weather, and almost half of them died.

Jacques Cartier made contact with the Haudenosaunee people as he explored the St. Lawrence River. However, the relationship ended in disaster due to Cartier's mistreatment of the Haudenosaunee leader.

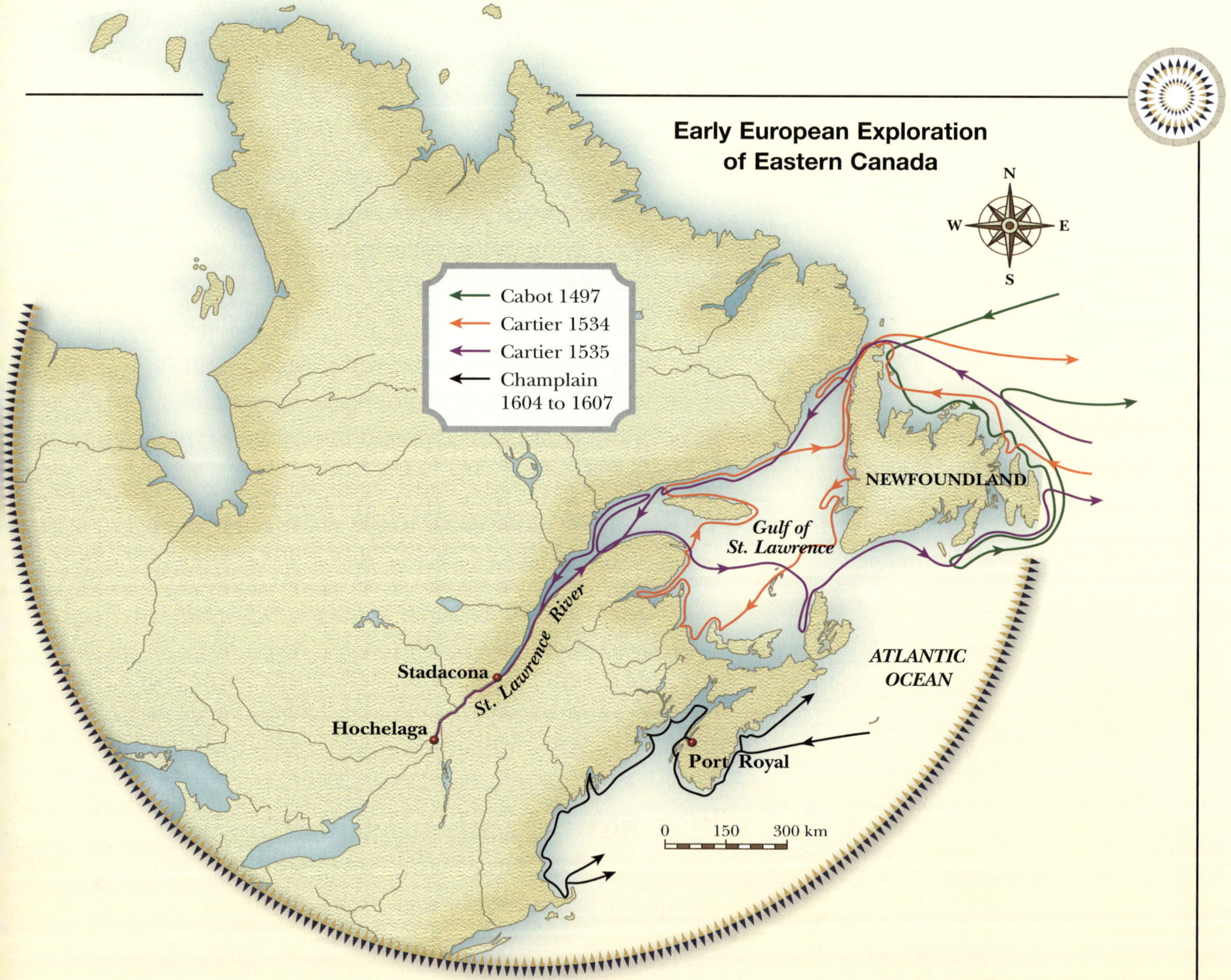

In the spring of 1605, Champlain helped to found Port Royal in what is now Nova Scotia. This was the first permanent French settlement in Canada. The settlers and French fishers traded metal goods with the Mi'kmaq people, who had beaver furs. Coats and hats made from beaver were very popular in Europe at the time, so the French could sell the furs for a high price.

In 1608, Champlain built a fort in what is now Québec City. This fort would become the centre of the fur trade. In later years, First Nations guides helped European explorers as they travelled west across Canada.

Reflect on

Strategies: How did using text features to make predictions help you understand what you were reading?

Critical Literacy: Think about the topic of first contact between First Nations and Europeans in North America. What different points of view could be used to present this topic?

Understanding media

Identifying Conventions and Techniques in Art

Art Speaks

One reason people create media texts is to share their ideas and feelings. A creator usually develops conventions, or a style, and techniques that match how he or she wants to communicate.

Look at this media work. Now read what the artist has to say about his work. What conventions and techniques does George Littlechild use? How do they make his art "speak"?

Four Buffalo Spirits

The mighty buffalo fed and clothed my ancestors. Millions of these magnificent animals once roamed the plains. By the end of the 1800s they were almost extinct – killed for money by the white men. This extermination was devastating to my ancestors who depended upon the buffalo for their very survival.

I painted four buffalo because four is a sacred number. These four represent the millions who have died. Four is also a healing number. It appears in all my work. There are four directions, four seasons, four elements, and four kinds of animals (those who walk, those who fly, those who swim, and those who crawl.)

Here is another work by George Littlechild. Study the art and read the explanation of how he created it. Thinking about the art on pages 81 and 83, how would you describe George Littlechild's conventions and techniques?

I Love the Moon, the Stars, and the Ancestors

I paint at night. I'm inspired to paint at night. I stand outside staring at the night sky and I begin to dream. The sky is like a doorway into the other world, the Spirit World.

I am inspired by the ancestors. When I look back on our history and see all the difficulties our ancestors had to face, I can only honor them. Through the wisdom of our Elders and the courage of all our people we have survived the past 500 years. I thank the Creator for *Wahkomkanak*, our ancestors.

In the center of this picture is Chief Joseph Samson. He wears an eagle headdress, the highest symbol in our culture. On the top and the sides of the picture are images of my great-great-grandfather, Louis Natuasis, who lived from 1858 to 1926. He was a headman to Chief Joseph Samson. He was born when my people were still free, when the buffalo still roamed.

In those days our Nation, the Plains Cree people, followed the buffalo in the spring and summer. In the winter we made camp by the rivers, which were the ancient roadways. The trees protected us from the snows and the winds. We hid in the valleys from our traditional enemies, the Blackfoot people.

G. Littlechild '91

Understanding reading strategies

Text Features: Visuals

Visual information includes maps, illustrations, timelines, diagrams, and photographs. Visuals work with text to give you another way of understanding what you read.

Searching for the Northwest Passage

By Vivien Bowers

Journey to the ends of the Earth! Like today's astronauts blasting off into unknown space, Arctic explorers sailed into treacherous, ice-choked waters, never knowing what lay ahead. Why? To find the Northwest Passage, that's why!

So Long, Cap'n Hudson

Europeans used to travel by land to trade in the Far East, but in the 1500s they started to look for a faster route. The Northwest Passage, an uncharted route through the Arctic waters of North America, looked like a possibility.

In 1611, the British explorer Henry Hudson figured he had found the Northwest Passage. (Yeah, right!) Actually, he was stuck in Hudson Bay. His starving, frostbitten crew wanted to go home, but Hudson was determined to keep looking. The crew mutinied; they took control of the ship and put Hudson, his teenage son, John, and all those who were sick into a small boat and set it adrift in the mist. The others sailed home, and Hudson was never seen again.

ARCTIC EXPLORATION: TO FIND THE NORTHWEST PASSAGE

Visuals may show something already explained in the text or they may provide additional information. Does this illustrated timeline explain what is in the text or give you additional information?

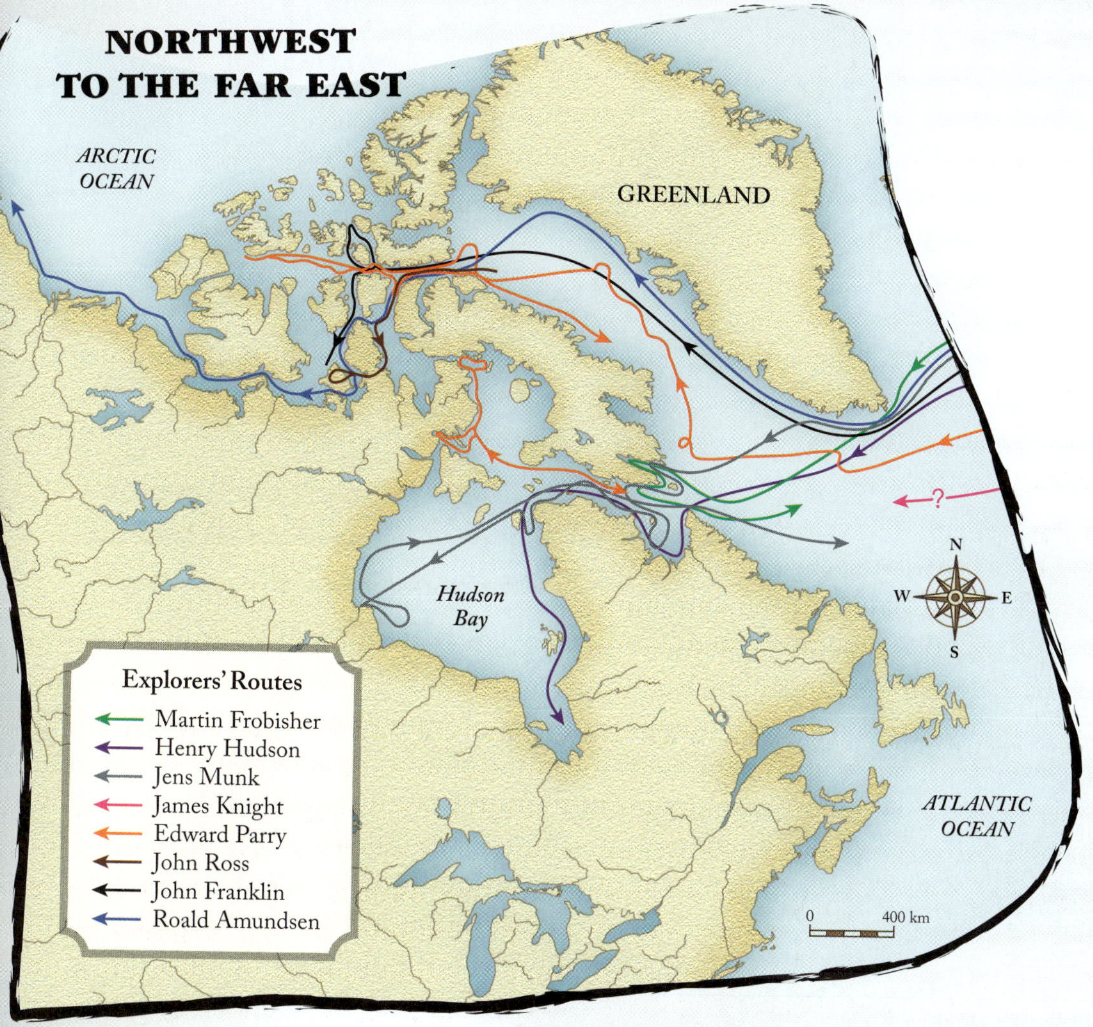

The Northwest Passage wound through the frozen islands of the Canadian Arctic. It never did become a popular travel route. Why might that be?

Sometimes a visual is the best way of giving information. How else could the writer have given the information in this map?

A visual is usually accompanied by a caption, or words that explain what the visual shows. What words on these two pages help you understand what the visuals are showing?

Scurvy and Other Delights of Foreign Travel

Exploring can be hazardous to your health! British expedition leaders usually hired twice as many sailors as they needed, figuring that half would die on the voyage. Often, they died of scurvy.

Grave stones mark the spot where the remains of two members of Franklin's crew were found in a lifeboat.

Visuals may show something already explained in the text or they may provide additional information. Why do you think the visual on this page was included?

Scurvy is caused by a lack of Vitamin C (found in fresh fruits and vegetables). Victims' gums bleed and rot, their teeth fall out, their swollen legs become covered with purple blotches, their joints ache, they lose weight, they're exhausted, and eventually they die.

Lost: John Franklin—Reward!

What happened to Sir John Franklin? It's one of the greatest mysteries in Canadian history.

Franklin's expedition sailed from England in 1845 in search of the Northwest Passage. But the 129 men in the crew disappeared off the face of the Earth! What went wrong? Over the next 10 years, 40 expeditions went looking for clues. (They mapped a lot of the Arctic while they were at it.)

Some searchers encountered Inuit carrying silver forks and spoons from Franklin's ships. These Inuit told stories of white men walking south and dropping from starvation. A bleached skeleton, dressed in fragments of a uniform, was found on King William Island, in today's Nunavut. A note inside a rock pile, apparently written more than two years into the expedition, said that the ships had been crushed in the ice and 24 men, including Franklin, were dead. The 105 survivors were walking south, according to the note, hoping to reach the nearest fur-trade fort. They were dragging heavy lifeboats on sledges, one of which was later discovered by searchers. It contained supplies (including silk handkerchiefs and button polish!) and two human skeletons.

Wilderness Survival

by Ann-Maureen Owens
and Jane Yealland

Would you eat your shoes if you were starving? That's what Arctic explorers had to do when they ran out of food. Surviving food shortages, harsh winters, and hordes of mosquitoes took skill and stamina.

Europeans who copied the Native ways of dealing with the dangers and problems of exploration had a better chance of making it in Canada. The explorers who continued to believe that they were superior and that Native people could not teach them anything often paid the ultimate price—losing their lives.

Applying Strategies

Text Features: Visuals

As you read this article, use visuals to help you understand what you are reading. Remember that a visual

- may show something already explained in the text or may provide additional information
- may be the best way of giving information
- is usually accompanied by a caption, or words that explain what it shows

Birchbark Canoes

When Samuel de Champlain arrived in Canada in 1603, he soon realized that the only way to explore its rivers and streams was by using Huron birchbark canoes. These light canoes could be paddled and portaged over shallow waters where bigger boats couldn't go.

Snowshoes

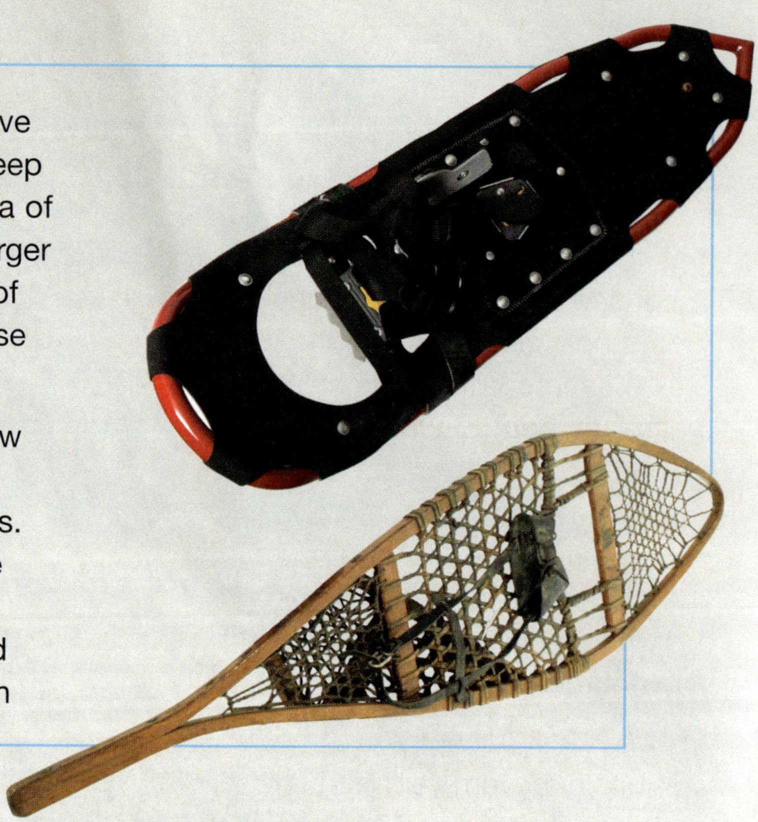

Snowshoes were used by almost every Native group in Canada. To keep from sinking in deep snow, the Native people used the clever idea of spreading a person's weight over an area larger than his or her foot. They based the shape of the snowshoe on animal tracks such as those made by bears, beavers, and foxes.

The size of the snowshoes depended on how deep the snow was and whether the Native people were hunting or carrying heavy packs. Ash or pine boughs were used for the frame and were held together by woven strips of rawhide. European explorers quickly realized snowshoes were an ideal way to get through heavy snow.

Toboggans

Toboggans, like snowshoes, were useful for moving people and supplies over snow. A toboggan was made from two pieces of birch lashed together with thongs of deerskin. If there was no wood, a frozen animal skin was used instead, and sometimes even a large piece of frozen meat.

Snowhouses

One danger of exploring in the Arctic was being caught in a sudden blizzard. The solution was to carve out blocks of snow and build a snowhouse, called an iglu by Inuit. A skilled builder could make one in 20 to 30 minutes. The heat created by people inside the iglu would melt the inside walls, which would then freeze into ice, making the snowhouse very strong.

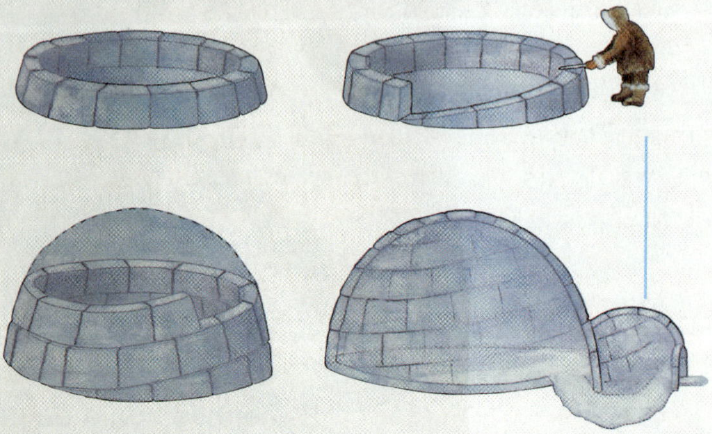

Caches

Sometimes explorers were travelling for months. They couldn't carry enough food for the return trip, so they copied the Native idea of storing food and supplies under large piles of rocks. These caches also served as landmarks. Explorer Robert Peary left several caches on his trek to the North Pole in 1909.

Did You Know?

Goggles with narrow slits carved by Inuit from whalebone were the earliest form of sunglasses. They protected Arctic travellers from snow blindness.

Pemmican

Pemmican, a Cree word meaning "greased food," was Canada's first fast food. Explorers often carried this Native food when travelling because it cut down on the need for hunting. Pemmican was made by drying bear, buffalo, or moose meat and pounding it into a powder, mixing it with berries and grease, then storing it in leather pouches.

Not only did just 1 kilogram of pemmican equal the amount of protein in 4 kilograms of fresh meat, it also wouldn't go bad. The Plains people produced and traded pemmican with the explorers and fur traders.

Rock Tripe

As well as eating animal skins and their own leather shoes when they were starving, explorers were often forced to eat a form of lichen (moss-like fungus) known as rock tripe. This plant, which grows on rocks in the Arctic, gave them enough protein to survive.

Rock tripe looks like dark lettuce and has a strong bitter taste. It must be boiled or its high acid content will upset starving stomachs. Hudson's Bay trader Samuel Hearne often ate rock tripe on his expedition to the Coppermine River in 1771.

Reflect on

Strategies: How did the visuals in this article help you understand what you were reading?

Connections: What experiences have you had with products that were invented by Aboriginal people?

Understanding writing strategies

Using Strong Transitions

Readers like text to be smooth just like skateboarders like the pavement to be smooth. You don't usually think about whether writing—or a sidewalk—is smooth, until you hit a bump.

Writers can smooth out their writing with transitions, or words that connect ideas. Transitions make it easy for readers to see how ideas flow from one sentence to the next, or from one paragraph to the next.

Read this section from *The Story of Canada* by Janet Lunn and Christopher Moore. The transitions are highlighted. Then try reading the section again, without the transitions. Notice how helpful the transitions are in showing the connections between ideas.

Rats, Weeds, and Viruses

When fishermen and explorers sailed from Europe to Canada, they brought small stowaways with them. Every ship had rats, and every time a ship was anchored in some sandy cove the rats had a chance to go ashore and discover the New World for themselves. Long before anyone from Europe settled in Canada, the rodents had scattered far and wide across the continent.

Rats were not the only animals aboard the ships. Soon pigs, horses, and cattle escaped to run wild in the new land. Plants arrived, too. Before the European ships came to this continent, there was not one dandelion in North America, but seeds crossed the ocean, stuck to a sailor's baggage or the mud of his boot. Once ashore, plants migrated faster than the humans they had come with. Today, if you collect ten different wild plants in a Canadian field, chances are that five will be the descendants of immigrants.

Much less welcome immigrants also found their way across the ocean. For thousands of years, Europe had shared its germs and diseases with Asia and Africa. The diseases were deadly, but over the centuries many people had built up some immunity to them. This meant that a disease might not infect everybody, or that it might weaken its victims but not kill them. In the Americas, where these diseases had never existed, none of the Aboriginal people were immune.

Like rats and dandelions, measles and fevers and tuberculosis and smallpox came on the ships. The sailors and explorers did not know about bacteria and viruses or how diseases spread, but spread they did. The microscopic newcomers passed from village to village, killing thousands of Aboriginal people. In some places, almost everyone in the village sickened and died, leaving too few to bury the dead. Across the Americas, as many as nine out of every ten people may have died from diseases. Nations collapsed.

Writers have many transitions to choose from. Different transitions do different jobs. The best transition is the one that shows how ideas connect. Here are some of the kinds of transitions you can use in your writing.

How Ideas Connect	Transitions
sequence	when, before, soon, today, after, now, then, later, first, second, next, finally
compare	too, also, like, in the same way, similarly
contrast	but, however, in contrast, still, yet, on the one hand … on the other hand
position	above, below, beyond, here, there, nearby, across, in front, in back
cause and effect	so, consequently, therefore, as a result, since, because, if, then, in order that
example	for example, for instance, specifically, according to
conclusion	finally, in conclusion, in the end, in summary

How to use strong transitions:

- ✔ Read your writing out loud. Mark places where you hear "bumps," or where the ideas do not connect smoothly.
- ✔ Think about how the ideas in sentences, or between paragraphs, are connected.
- ✔ Add transitions that match your ideas.
- ✔ Read your writing out loud again. Ask yourself, "Does my writing read smoothly? Will readers understand how my ideas are connected?"

Strangers on the Coast

by Janet Lunn and Christopher Moore

Applying Strategies

Reading Like a Writer

As you read, identify strong transitions. Notice how the writers use transitions to show how ideas are connected and to make the writing read smoothly.

On a day in late summer, a thousand years ago, Leif Ericsson gripped the tiller of his wave-skimming ship. To the west, there it was, rising from the ocean like a great humpback whale—the land Bjarni had told them about!

Leif Ericsson's people were the Norse from Scandinavia, in the north of Europe, and everyone in Europe feared them. From Russia to the Mediterranean Sea, the fierce Norse went raiding in their longships, sculpted dragons pointing the way. The Norse word *viking*, which means "raiding," became the name others used for them. But the Vikings were bold explorers, too. At a time when most European sailors hardly dared go beyond their own shores, the Norse had sailed as far as Iceland and settled there. Leif's own father, Eric the Red, had sailed farther west, to Greenland.

Soon after Eric the Red had sailed to Greenland, a merchant named Bjarni Herjolfsson was sailing to Greenland and got caught by a howling storm. The storm carried him far to the west and he sighted a forested land. When he finally reached the Greenland port, Bjarni told his story. Leif, whose friends called him Leif the Lucky, was fascinated by the story. He bought Bjarni's ship, repaired it, and went with his crew in search of the unknown land.

The Viking raiders were fierce in battle.

The Norse boldly explored west.

Now, on a late summer day, Leif was lucky indeed to find the land Bjarni had seen. The tired, salt-caked adventurers waded ashore on an island off this unfamiliar coast. A Norse storyteller wrote in the *Saga of the Greenlanders* that "They touched the dew with their hands and they thought they had never known anything to taste so sweet." The Norse had come to North America.

When they pulled their ship ashore on the mainland, Leif's crew found a land that was everything they had hoped for. According to the *Saga*, they saw salmon in the rivers "bigger than any they had ever seen before." Deep forests covered the hills. And one of the crew even came back from exploring with what looked like grapes and vines. What a marvellous country, far richer than cold Greenland! Leif named it "Vinland the Good" and decided to spend the winter. He set the men to building huts. The *Saga* says there was no frost that winter, and the cattle the Norse had brought in their ship were able to graze outdoors.

The following spring, Leif loaded his ship with timber and sailed back to Greenland. Soon there were new expeditions setting out for Vinland.

Viking longships, with their fierce dragonhead prows, could reach speeds of up to 35 km per hour.

The next year, Leif's brother Thorvald led an expedition. But his was not as lucky as Leif's. One day, Thorvald and his men found strangers sleeping under upturned kayaks. The Norse killed eight of these strangers, Aboriginal men, but one escaped and soon returned with many more men in kayaks. Thorvald's men fought them from their longship, sheltering behind a row of shields, but an arrow flew between the shields and struck Thorvald. He realized that he was going to die. "We have found a good country," he said, "but we will not be able to benefit from it." His men buried him and went home.

A year or so later, Thorfinn Karlsefni led a large fleet from Greenland to the "good country," carrying 250 men and women. They spent several years there, living in houses of sod and stone to keep out the cold winds that raged across the land. Their sheep and goats grazed on the natural meadows. They made rough clothing from the sheep's wool and drank nourishing goat milk. The first winter, Thorfinn's wife, Gudrid, gave birth to a baby boy named Snorri—the first child of Europeans born in North America.

In 1960, the remains of a Norse settlement were found at L'Anse aux Meadows, on the island now called Newfoundland. Now there are three reconstructed Norse buildings for visitors to explore. Some archaeologists think this might be where Thorfinn, Gudrid, and Snorri lived.

The winter was harsh. People grew hungry and sick, and they fought with each other. They also met the Native people of the land. The Norse called them Skraelings, and fought with them. The Skraelings fought back, and soon the settlers were afraid to stay in this new land. Snorri was three years old when the expedition returned to Greenland.

After that, Norse sailors seldom visited the land west of Greenland. The seas were rough, the climate was getting colder, and the Skraelings fought hard to defend their land. In Greenland, the cold and lonely Norse settlements slowly dwindled away, defeated by the worsening climate. The Norse retreated, moving back east to Iceland or the countries of their ancestors: Norway, Sweden, and Denmark.

So the Vikings no longer went to Vinland the Good and remembered it only in the stories they told at night in the great halls of Scandinavia. And it would be hundreds of years before Europeans returned to the shores of Canada.

Archaeologists found this bone needle and other sewing tools at L'Anse aux Meadows. They were left behind by the Vikings who once lived on "Vinland."

Reflect on

Strategies: Find three strong transitions. What kinds of transitions did you find? How do they show the connections between ideas?

Your Learning: Think about what you have learned about the Vikings. What new questions do you have about the history of the Norse? Where can you look for answers to your questions?

FUR TRADING

by Charlotte Gray and Sara Angel

Putting It All Together

As you read, remember to use the strategies you learned in this unit.

- Predict using text features.
- Use visuals to help you understand what you are reading.
- Identify strong transitions.

How It Began

Long before Europeans visited Canada's shores, the Aboriginal peoples of North America traded furs and other goods with each other, often over great distances. The first outsiders to trade for furs were the sailors who came ashore on the Atlantic Coast in the 1500s, to dry the fish they had caught. The furs they took home to Europe sold for high prices, especially after the wide-brimmed felt hat became fashionable in the late 1500s. Beaver pelts made the best felt, but Europe had already used up most of its own beaver population.

IN CANADA

Expanding Trade

Over time, this huge demand for beaver pelts in Europe helped establish permanent settlement in what is now Canada. In the early 1600s, the French set up trading posts at Port Royal, Tadoussac, and Québec—mainly as bases for the fur trade. By the 1660s, the French had established a trading network protected by a system of forts that extended to the limits of the St. Lawrence and the Great Lakes. Later, the Hudson's Bay Company (HBC) was created and it set up its own network of fur trade posts.

These trading posts were among the hundreds that developed during the fur trade.

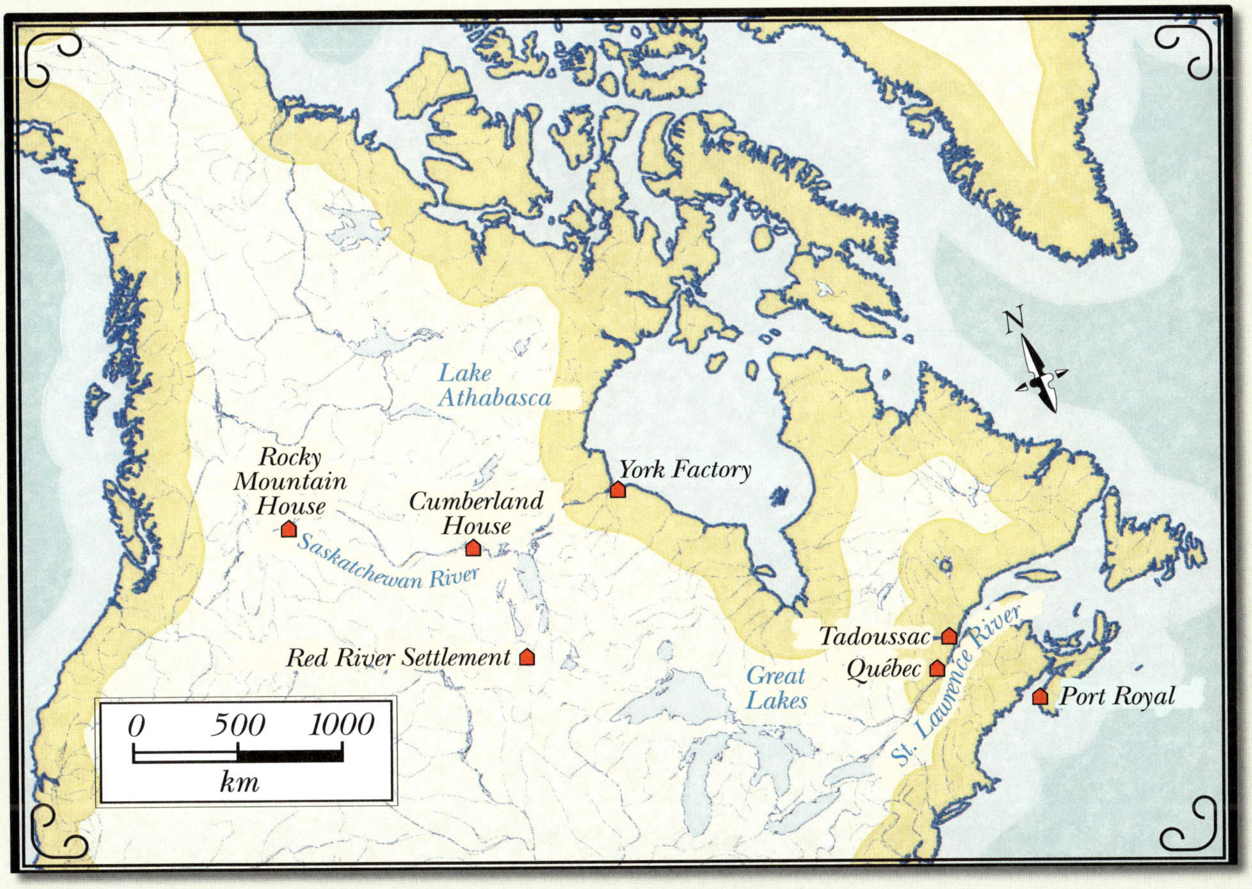

The Beaver Felt Hat

To make a beaver felt hat, first, the coarse outer hairs were removed from the beaver pelts. Then, the short, barbed underfur of the beaver was made into a soft, durable, warm, and water-resistant felt. Finally, the felt was shaped into the popular hats.

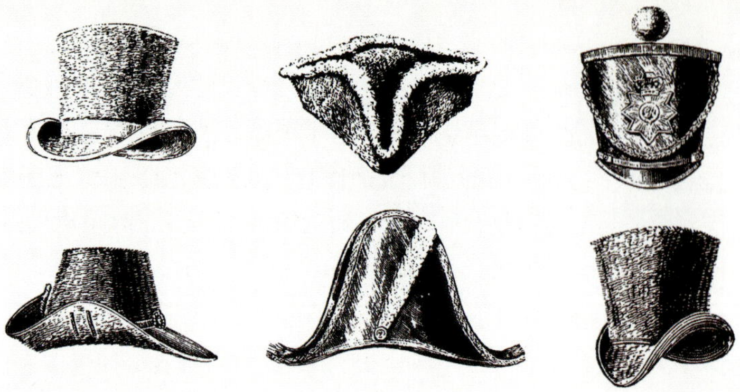

For roughly 300 years, from the mid-1500s to the mid-1800s, beaver hats stayed in fashion. During this time, almost every North American beaver pelt sold to European traders ended up as beaver felt for hats.

One side of this coin, from 1854, shows the symbol of the HBC; the other side shows that the coin is worth "one made beaver" (1MB).

Like Money

In the area controlled by the Hudson's Bay Company (HBC), beaver pelts were like money. In fact, one top-quality beaver pelt in good condition (called "one made beaver") became the standard unit, like a dollar today. Eventually, the HBC started making coins or tokens to represent the currency. Today in Canada, the beaver still appears as a symbol on many things—including coins.

Exploring and Mapping

As the HBC set up and expanded its network of fur trade posts, its employees travelled huge distances to explore the land, map it, and trade for furs. In the late 1700s and early 1800s, Peter Fidler was one explorer and trader with the HBC. Peter travelled about 76 000 km for his work, and his Cree wife, Mary, often travelled with him. Peter and Mary had 14 children, who became part of the Métis community in the Red River settlement (near where Winnipeg stands today).

Over the years, Peter listed the date, time, and location of each child's birth in his notebook. In 1802, Mary gave birth to their fourth child, Valery, after a long trip from a trading post on the Saskatchewan River north to the shores of Lake Athabasca. It took Mary, Peter, and 17 other HBC employees 43 days by birchbark canoe, with countless portages.

5 Almanacks — 4.5
4 15 1
1820 July 2 6 pm Norway Ho. Peter
1822 July 9 Harriet
1819 June 18 Maryet — died July 21 8.55 pm
1795 June 20 — 0. 8 Thomas York Factory
1798 Octr 10 — 12.35 Charles Cumberland
1800 Novr 10 — 12.15 George Chesterfield ho
1802 Novr 26 2. 3 Valey Nott. house
1804 Octr 12. 15.42 Secus ooggan Nott
1806 Novr 29 22 50 andrew Cumb House
1809 June 17 4 0 alban Holy Lake
1811 June 27 20. 2 Mary Chat. Norta
1813 augt 26 0 45 Faith at Slater
River Died at Brandon House 6 oct at noon
Secusoggan died 1814 march 7th 8am — ill 24 Days
1814 Novr 24 8 30 Clement Brandon
1817 March 5 11. 10 Colette Halketts House

from the notebook of Peter Fidler

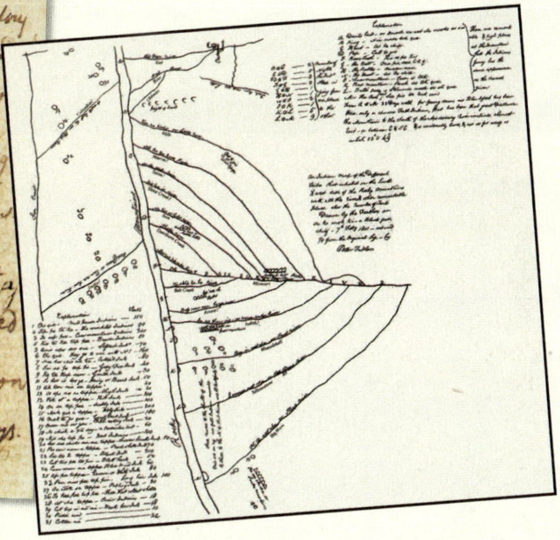

Peter Fidler's sketch of Akka Makkoye's map

While the fur trade grew, Mary Fidler and many other Aboriginal people helped HBC workers in their travels. In 1801, a Siksika leader named Akka Makkoye drew a map in the snow and earth for Peter Fidler. Peter sketched the map and sent it to his HBC bosses, who then sent it to London, England. In London, a mapmaker named Aaron Arrowsmith used Akka Makkoye's map. Arrowsmith's maps were used by European explorers for many years to come.

The Decline of the Fur Trade

By the 1860s, the fur trade was becoming less and less important. The beaver hat wasn't fashionable anymore and settlers were moving into the territories that the HBC used to control.

This 1869 painting by Frances Anne Hopkins shows HBC workers, her husband (an HBC boss), and herself.

When the beaver felt trade finally died out, life did not return to what it had been in the 1500s. The trade had brought many Aboriginal peoples and newcomers into contact, established permanent European settlements in Canada, and changed life here forever.

In 1856, the Dutch painter Cornelius Krieghoff painted this scene of farm life in Quebec.

Reflect on

Strategies: How did text features and visuals help you learn about the fur trade as you were reading this article?

Connections: What fashions are popular in Canada today? Do you think any of these fashions could change our way of life for centuries to come?

Your Choices

In this unit, you will

- find important ideas and supporting details
- summarize important information in conversations
- identify characteristics of cause-and-effect text pattern
- write an organized paragraph
- interpret public service ads
- learn about healthy choices

LET'S TALK

Choosing Health

What choices do you see being made in these photos?

Understanding reading strategies

Finding Important Ideas

Finding important ideas and identifying, or citing, supporting details helps you think about and understand what you are reading.

Titles and headings often give an overview of important ideas. Use them to decide what might be the important ideas in this article.

Operation Brainwash

by Ann Douglas and Julie Douglas

Important ideas can be found anywhere in a section, or implied. Where is the important idea in this section?

Supporting details help to explain important ideas. What details explain why the writers say "there's something wrong with our beauty standards"?

Media and Body Image

By the time you start high school, you will have been exposed to 350 000 television and print advertisements, over 50 percent of which stress being beautiful and thin. Talk about being brainwashed! To make matters worse, many of the images have been altered. If even supermodels need to have their pictures "fixed" to take out pimples and wrinkles, there's something wrong with our beauty standards, don't you think?

Of course, it can be fun to paint your nails, colour your hair, and play around with your appearance. Unfortunately, many of the ads about these beauty products lose sight of the fact that using these products is supposed to be a fun way of expressing yourself—not something you have to do in order to measure up to someone else's beauty idea.

How It Works

Women's magazines are known for sandwiching articles on dieting between recipes for chocolate cake, or placing an article on eating disorders across from an ad designed to play on insecurities you may have about your body.

And how do magazines affect young readers? A recent study showed that 69 percent of girls base their ideal body image on pictures they see in magazines, and 47 percent say that looking at these images makes them want to lose weight.

Important ideas can be stated anywhere in a section, or implied. How do supporting details help you figure out the implied important idea in this section?

Fighting Back

You can fight back against negative media images. For example, if you come across an ad that really offends you, write a letter to the company that produced the ad and send a copy of your letter to the magazine or newspaper that printed the ad or the television station that aired it. And the next time you're standing in line at the store looking at the magazines, be choosy. Don't automatically spend your money on the one featuring an article on weight loss or on making yourself look more beautiful. Don't give in to our culture's fixation with weight and beauty.

Important ideas can be stated anywhere in a section, or implied. How do supporting details help you figure out the important idea in this section?

An important idea can be developed over several paragraphs. What are the supporting details on this page? What important idea do the details support?

You can also ask questions about images. Look at the different ways that girls and women are depicted in ads in magazines. In what ways do the "ideal" girls and women in these ads compare to photos of real girls and women you know?

Listen carefully to the types of words television advertisers use to convince you to buy their products. Is their goal to make you feel worse about yourself or to convince you that their products will make you feel better about yourself? Or both?

You can also fight for positive images. Help spread the word about positive body image. Get your friends talking about what they see in the media. Make sure they realize that they don't have to take all those advertising messages at face value. If you find an ad that makes you feel good, consider writing to that manufacturer. Better yet, ask your health teacher if you can set up a Hall of Fame wall in your classroom to spotlight all the positive ads you find in newspapers and magazines.

Finally, make a list of all the women you admire. These could be people you know in real life or women you've read about in newspapers or seen on TV. Think about why you admire them. Is it their looks, their achievements, or their personalities that you find inspiring?

The Babysitter's Start-up Guide

by Cathy Rondina

Are you thinking about becoming a babysitter? If so, great! Babysitting can earn you a little extra money and provide an important service for people in your community. This guide is designed to help you get started.

The Job

Being a babysitter means that you are taking care of children while their parents are away. Babysitting can be fun and rewarding, but it's also a big responsibility that must be taken seriously.

Getting Ready

Before you jump into babysitting, here are a few things to consider:

Your Interests

If the idea of being alone with a couple of kids doesn't sound like fun, this probably isn't the job for you. And that's OK. But if you enjoy being around kids, just remember:

- Your job wouldn't be just to hang out with the kids; you need to *look after* them.
- Kids come in all different shapes and sizes. If changing smelly diapers grosses you out, think about babysitting only older kids.

Applying Strategies

Finding Important Ideas

As you read, identify important ideas and supporting details to help you think about what you are reading. Remember that

- titles and headings can give an overview of important ideas
- supporting details help explain important ideas
- important ideas can be anywhere in a section, or implied
- important ideas can be developed over several paragraphs

Your Family

Babysitting takes babysitters away from their own families. You need your family's permission in order to say OK to any babysitting. Talk about and agree on the details. For example, are you allowed to babysit on a school night? After midnight? When would it be OK to walk home from a babysitting job and when should you get a ride?

Your Time

The great thing about babysitting is that it can work well for kids going to school. But, do you really have enough time? Sit down and write a schedule of what you do every week—including homework *and* skating lessons, soccer practice, or whatever else you're involved in. Look at your schedule and decide if you have time—and if so, when and how much time. And, sure, you might be able to sneak in a little study time while babysitting, but don't count on it!

Your Readiness

If you sometimes take care of yourself at home or you look after younger brothers or sisters, you might be ready for a babysitting job. If you haven't spent much time around younger kids, you need to get some experience first. For example, you could volunteer to help your neighbour or family friends with their young kids.

Here are some more ways to help you get ready for babysitting:

- Take a babysitting course—for example, at the local library or community centre.
- Talk to parents who hire babysitters.
- Talk to other kids who are babysitters.
- Use your library and the Internet to read all you can about child care and first aid.

If You Think You're Ready

If you're still interested and want to give babysitting a try, then it's time to think about preparing for and getting the jobs. Take care and have fun!

Reflect on

Strategies: How did identifying important ideas and supporting details help you think about babysitting as a job?

Critical Literacy: Whose point of view might be missing from this article? What important ideas might that person want to add?

Summarizing Important Information in Conversations

You have conversations every day. Occasionally, you receive a lot of information that is important for you to understand and remember. For example, you might receive information about changes on your sports team, or about a job someone needs you to do.

Using your listening and speaking skills will help you summarize important information.

How to summarize important information in conversations:

- ✔ Ask questions to clarify your understanding.
- ✔ Focus on identifying big ideas.
- ✔ Check your understanding by restating important information.
- ✔ If possible, jot down your summary while the ideas are fresh in your mind.

Understanding text patterns

Identifying Characteristics of Cause-and-Effect Text Pattern

Writers use cause-and-effect text pattern to explain why things happen. Cause-and-effect text pattern has certain characteristics:

- The text answers the question "why?"
- Ideas are linked to show that one thing (the cause) makes something else (the effect) happen.
- One cause can have several effects.
- One effect can have several causes.

The text answers the question "why?" Preview the title and headings in this article. What do you expect this article to explain?

The "What" and "Why" of Self-Esteem

Written by KidsHealth
Illustrated by Ian Kim

You can't touch it, but it affects how you feel. You can't see it, but it's there when you look at yourself in the mirror. You can't hear it, but it's there every time you talk about yourself. What is this important but mysterious thing? It's your self-esteem!

What Is Self-Esteem?

To understand self-esteem, it helps to break the term into two words. Let's take a look at the word esteem first. Esteem (say: ess-teem) is a fancy word for thinking that someone or something is important, or valuing that person or thing. For example, if you really admire your friend's dad because he volunteers at the fire department, it means you hold him in high esteem. And the special trophy for the most valuable player on a team is often called an esteemed trophy. This means the trophy stands for an important accomplishment.

And self means, well, yourself! So, put the two words together and it's easier to see what self-esteem is. It's how much you value yourself and how important you think you are. It's how you see yourself and how you feel about your achievements.

Self-esteem isn't bragging about how great you are. It's more like quietly knowing that you're worth a lot (priceless, in fact!). It's not about thinking you're perfect—because nobody is—but about knowing that you're worthy of being loved and accepted.

Why Self-Esteem Is Important

Self-esteem isn't like a cool pair of running shoes that you'd love to have but don't have to have. A kid needs to have self-esteem. Good self-esteem is important because it helps you to hold your head high and feel proud of yourself and of what you can do. It gives you the courage to try new things and the power to believe in yourself. It lets you respect yourself, even when you make mistakes. And when you respect yourself, adults and other kids usually respect you, too.

Having good self-esteem is also the ticket to making good choices about your mind and body. If you think you're important, you'll be less likely to follow the crowd if your friends are doing something dumb or dangerous. If you have good self-esteem, you know that you're smart enough to make your own decisions. You value your safety, your feelings, your health—your whole self! Good self-esteem helps you know that every part of you is worth caring for and protecting.

One cause can have several effects. What are some effects of good self-esteem?

How Kids Get Self-Esteem

Babies don't see themselves in a good or bad way. They don't think "I'm great!" when they let out a big burp, or "Oh, no, this diaper makes my legs look weird!" Instead, people around a baby help him or her develop self-esteem. How? By encouraging the baby when he or she learns to crawl, walk, or talk. They often say, "Good job. Good for you!" When people take good care of a baby, that also helps him or her feel lovable and valuable.

One effect can have several causes. What causes kids to develop good self-esteem?

As kids get older, they can have a bigger role in developing their self-esteem. Achievements—like getting a good grade on a test or making the All-Star soccer team—are things kids can be proud of. So is having a good sense of humour or being a good friend.

A kid's family and other people in his or her life—like coaches, teammates, and classmates—also can boost his or her self-esteem. They can help a kid figure out how to do things or they can notice his or her good qualities. They can believe in the kid and encourage him or her to try again when something doesn't go right the first time. It's all part of kids learning to see themselves in a positive way, to feel proud of what they've done, and to be confident that there's a lot more they can do.

A Little on Low Self-Esteem

Maybe you know kids with low self-esteem, kids who don't think very highly of themselves or seem to criticize themselves too much. Or maybe you have low self-esteem and don't always feel very good about yourself or think you're important.

Sometimes a kid will have low self-esteem if family members don't encourage him or her enough, or if there is a lot of yelling at home. Other times, a kid's self-esteem can be hurt in the classroom. Someone at school might make a kid feel dumb, or perhaps there is a bully who says hurtful things.

Ideas are linked to show that one thing (the cause) makes something else (the effect) happen. What causes does the text link to the effect of low self-esteem?

For some kids, classes at school can seem so hard that they can't keep up or get the grades they'd hoped for. This situation can make them feel bad about themselves and hurt their self-esteem. Their self-esteem will improve when a teacher, tutor, or counsellor encourages them, is patient, and helps them get back on track with learning. When they start to do well, their self-esteem will skyrocket!

And there are some kids who have good self-esteem but then something happens to change that, for example:

- If a kid moves and doesn't make friends right away at the new school, he or she might start to feel bad.
- A kid whose parents divorce also may find that this can affect self-esteem. He or she may feel unlovable or to blame for the divorce.
- A kid who feels too fat or too thin may start thinking that means he or she isn't good enough.
- Even going through the body changes of puberty—something that everybody does—can affect a kid's self-esteem.

The text answers the question "why?" Why do some kids with good self-esteem change and seem to lose their positive feelings?

The text answers the question "why?" Why is it important to have good self-esteem as you get older?

One effect can have several causes. What actions can cause an increase in your self-esteem? Look for causes on this page and the next page.

Boosting Your Self-Esteem

Of course it's OK to have ups and downs in your feelings, but having low self-esteem isn't OK. Feeling like you're not important can make you sad and can keep you from trying new things. It can keep you from making friends or hurt how you do at school. Having strong self-esteem is also a very big part of growing up. As you get older and face tough decisions—especially under peer pressure—the more self-esteem you have, the better. It's important to know you're worth a lot.

If you think you might have low self-esteem, try talking to an adult you trust about it. He or she may be able to help you come up with some good ideas for building your self-esteem.

In the meantime, here are a few things that you can try to increase your self-esteem:

- Make a list of the stuff you're good at. It can be anything from drawing or singing to playing a sport or telling a good joke. If you're having trouble with your list, ask your mom or dad to help you with it. Then add a few things to the list that you'd like to be good at. Your mom or dad can help you plan a way to work on those skills or talents.

- Give yourself three compliments every day. Don't just say, "I'm so great." Be specific about something good about yourself, like, "I was a good friend to Jill today" or "I did better on that test than I thought I would." While you're at it, before you go to bed every night, list three things in your day that really made you happy.
- Remember that your body is your own, no matter what shape, size, or colour it is. If you are worried about your weight or size, you can check with your doctor to make sure that things are OK. Remind yourself of things about your body that are cool, like, "My legs are strong and I can skate really well."
- Remember that there are things about yourself you can't change. You should accept and love these things—such as skin colour and shoe size—because they are part of you.
- When you hear negative comments in your head, tell yourself to stop. This takes power away from the voice inside that discourages you.

By focusing on the good things you do and all your great qualities, you learn to love and accept yourself—the main ingredients for strong self-esteem! Even if you've got room for improvement (and who doesn't?), realizing that you're valuable and important helps your self-esteem to shine.

FOOD ALLERGIES

Written by Diane Swanson
Illustrated by Rose Cowles

Applying Strategies

As you read, identify characteristics of cause-and-effect text pattern to help you understand what you are reading:

- The text answers the question "why?"
- Ideas are linked to show that one thing (the cause) makes something else (the effect) happen.
- One cause can have several effects.
- One effect can have several causes.

For most people, whole-wheat bread, peanut butter, and milk make a healthy choice for lunch. But for someone with food allergies, they could be a recipe for serious illness or even death. That's why some schools try to be as "peanut free" as possible, and many food packages and restaurant menus contain ingredient warnings—to help people with allergies avoid danger. You can help, too, by being aware of family or friends who have allergies, understanding why food allergies occur, and learning which foods are the most common triggers.

Case of Mistaken Identity

Card playing usually isn't considered dangerous, but one man was attacked by food while having a game with his son. Hours earlier, the man's son had snacked on some shrimp, which his father was highly allergic to. As they were playing cards, traces of the shrimp passed from the son's hands to the cards, then the father's hands. When the man casually rubbed his eyes, the shrimp entered his body. That's all it took to set off an allergic reaction.

A food allergy is really a case of mistaken identity. The body wrongly labels one or more of the proteins in a particular food as an enemy invader. The immune system—special cells that fight germs, viruses and bacteria—jumps into action, sending proteins called antibodies to search for the invader. Then it releases chemicals to destroy the enemy.

The problem is that these chemicals irritate parts of the body, such as the digestive system. Swelling, vomiting, and diarrhea are common reactions. They can be mild or severe, but fortunately they aren't usually very strong the first time people eat food they're allergic to.

The Offenders

Almost any kind of food can produce an allergic reaction, but most of the trouble comes from the proteins in cow's milk, wheat, egg whites, soya beans, nuts (especially peanuts), fish, and shellfish (shrimp, crab, lobster). People with food allergies are often allergic to two or three different foods and to some non-foods, such as pollen and dust.

Food allergies can be so strong that contact with just 0.001 mL (1/5000 tsp.) of the offending food can cause death within 15 minutes. Up to eight percent of children have food allergies, but many outgrow them. Only about two percent of adults have true food allergies.

There is no cure for food allergies, so people who suffer from them must be very careful to avoid foods that trigger attacks.

You Try It

People with food allergies must read product labels carefully. Their lives may depend on it. The labels are supposed to list everything that the products contain.

Check the contents of your fridge and kitchen cupboards. See how many labels list ingredients that commonly cause problems for people with food allergies—milk, wheat flour, egg whites, soya beans, or nuts. These ingredients can pop up in some unexpected places.

Can you spot any labels that include special warnings for people with food allergies?

Reflect on

Strategies: How did identifying cause-and-effect relationships help you understand the important ideas in this article?

Your Learning: How might remembering what you learned from this article be helpful to you in the future?

Understanding writing strategies

Writing an Organized Paragraph

A paragraph develops a single idea. Most of what we read and write is presented in paragraphs. An organized paragraph is clear, informative, and interesting.

Read this paragraph from Shari Graydon's book *Made You Look: How Advertising Works and Why You Should Know.* The text is taken from a section called "Who Knew? Clever Campaigns Create New Needs." Think about how she organized her paragraph.

Do you know how diamonds came to be the gem of choice for engagement rings? You might imagine that it's a centuries-old tradition handed down for generations. In fact, diamond engagement rings are an invention of advertising. For centuries, opals, rubies, and sapphires were considered much more exotic than diamonds, and more often featured in women's engagement rings. But in 1947, the big diamond producer De Beers began advertising the glittering white stones as the symbol of love. The company's slogan, "Diamonds are forever," cleverly linked the hardness and durability of diamonds with the notion of permanent love, and diamonds quickly became "the" gem to use in engagement rings. Isn't it strange that a few words, repeated many times, can change how people think and act?

How to write an organized paragraph:

- ✔ Decide on your purpose and audience.
- ✔ Begin with a strong lead.
- ✔ Present a strong main idea with supporting details.
- ✔ End with a strong conclusion.

Reading the Signals

by Ann Douglas and Julie Douglas

Applying Strategies

Reading Like a Writer

As you read this article, think about how each paragraph is organized. Figure out the writers' purpose and audience. Notice the lead and conclusion. Identify the main idea and supporting details that make each paragraph clear and informative.

The best way to eat is the one that comes naturally: paying attention to your body's hunger and fullness "signals." Your body is equipped to tell you when it's time to eat—your stomach feels slightly empty and you start thinking about food. Your body can also tell you when it's time to put on the brakes. If you start feeling full in the middle of dinner, your body is letting you know it's time to give your fork a rest. Read the signals!

If you ignore the signals, your body will react. If you ignore your body's hunger signals, it will try even harder to get your attention. You'll start feeling light-headed, you'll have difficulty concentrating on anything but food, and you'll develop a killer headache. When you finally give in to your hunger pangs, chances are you'll go overboard, stuffing your face with any food that isn't nailed down. And, if you ignore your body's fullness signals, you'll also experience some physical discomfort. Your stomach will start feeling overly full, you may start to feel sick, and you'll be more inclined to flop out on the couch than to hop on your bike or skateboard. Neither extreme is comfortable.

To get more in touch with your body's signals, check out the handy Hunger Scale on the opposite page. Don't be surprised if your food intake varies a bit from day to day: you'll likely have days when you are positively ravenous and other days when you couldn't care less about food. What matters is that you let your body's appetite guide you instead of going by anybody else's ideas about how much you should—or shouldn't—be eating.

HUNGER SCALE: How You're Feeling

+5 **Stuffed** You've made too many trips to the all-you-can-eat buffet. You feel so tired and stuffed you'd like nothing more than to take a nap. Groan!

+4 **Stomach Bulging** You've eaten so much food your stomach feels uncomfortably full. It might even hurt. You're already wishing you had passed up that third piece of cake.

+3 **Bloated** You feel bloated and uncomfortable. Suddenly, your jeans feel too tight. Could they have shrunk in the dryer?

+2 **More Than Satisfied** Your stomach is saying, "No," but your mind is telling you "Yes" to a few more bites, even though you're no longer really tasting your food.

+1 **Just a Bit Over** You may have overindulged a bit, but you stopped before you got too uncomfortable. You may even have managed to leave something on your plate.

✓ **Satisfied** You're content, happy, and energized. You're neither stuffed nor starving, so you're able to focus on things other than food. Right on!

-1 **Mild Hunger** It's been three or four hours since you last ate. You've got a mild hollow feeling in your stomach and you're starting to think about food. Where did you leave that granola bar?

-2 **Thinking About Food** You're hungry enough to fantasize about food. Hope your teacher isn't giving hints about the big test coming up, because you're not really paying attention!

-3 **Empty** Your urge to eat is so strong you can't think of anything but filling the hollow pit in your stomach. It's almost impossible to concentrate on anything around you.

-4 **Famished** Your stomach is rumbling and you've become irritable and cranky. Anyone who gets between you and the vending machine is in trouble! You're starting to feel weak and nauseous.

-5 **Too Far Gone** You have a headache, you feel dizzy, and you've lost your coordination. You've gone so long without food that you're too tired to eat. All you want to do is go to sleep.

Reflect on

Strategies: How does thinking about the writing of others help you make your own writing effective? What did you notice in this article that will help you draft or revise a paragraph?

Your Learning: What did you learn that can help you support a friend or family member who is worried about eating too much or too little?

Understanding media

Interpreting Messages in Public Service Ads

What's the Message?

Not all advertisements are trying to sell you something. The aim of some ads is to inform you about public services or programs. No matter their goal, all ads are designed to catch your attention and give you a powerful message. Your task is to figure out what that message is.

An overt message states information directly. Read the print on this ad to learn what organization created the ad and why.

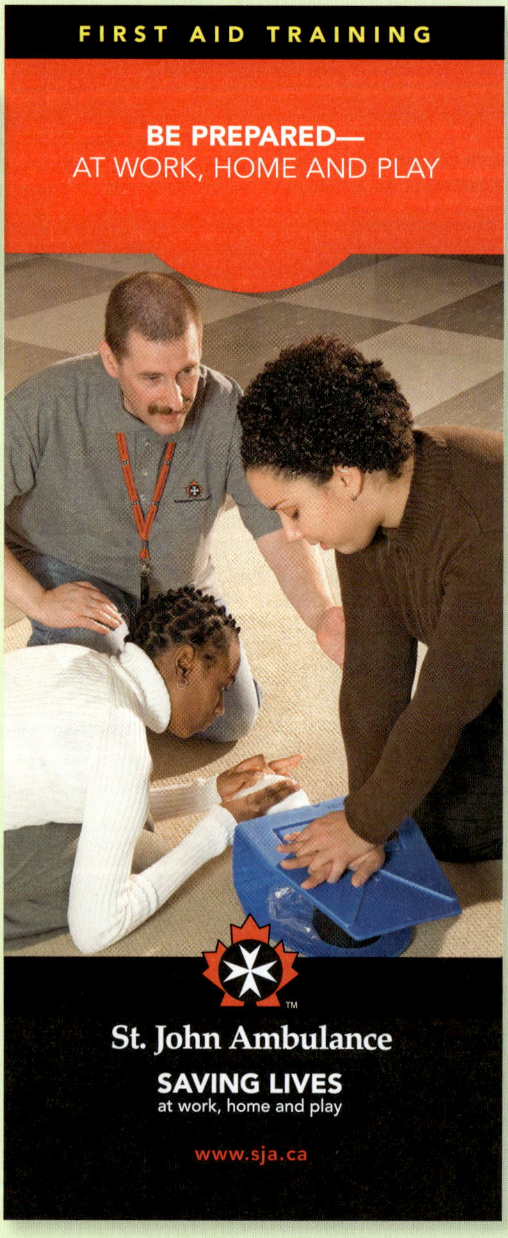

An implied message gives you an impression or a feeling. What does the photo in this ad show? What impression does it give you about first aid training?

To interpret the message in an ad, combine the overt and implied messages. What is your interpretation of the message in this ad? What do the creators want you to do or believe?

Figure out the overt and implied messages in this ad. What's your interpretation of the message in the ad? What do the creators want you to do or believe?

Safe and Smiling ~in~ THE GREAT OUTDOORS

by Laura Edlund

Putting It All Together

As you read this article, remember to use the strategies you learned in this unit:

- Find important ideas and supporting details.
- Identify characteristics of cause-and-effect text pattern.
- Notice how paragraphs are organized.

Are you tired of breathing stuffy indoor air? Would you like a change of scenery and a chance to stretch your legs? Try exploring the great outdoors and see what nature has to offer. But before you strap on that backpack, remember that while getting active in nature can be lots of fun, it also requires you to act responsibly. Why? Planning, preparing, and paying attention will keep you safe and allow you to make the most of your outing.

PLAN IT

A day hike could turn very scary—and dangerous!—if it gets dark before you've finished the trail. You can avoid such a situation by planning your trip. This involves deciding the "where," "when," and "how" of your outing. That is, figure out where you are going, when and for how long you are going, and how you will get there and back. Be specific. For example, Kevin's plan "hike in the woods with Sujay" was too vague, so he refined it: "Bike to Sujay's and ride with him to Lighthouse Park, hike the Lookout Trail, and ride home by 5 p.m." A clear, specific plan will help you stay safe and avoid disappointments.

Once you have your plan set, spread the word. Make sure a responsible adult who is not going on the outing knows the plan. Some parks even ask that you tell the warden your plan before you set off on your trip. That way, if you do have an emergency, someone will know when and where to send help.

PREPARE FOR IT

Once you have a plan, you can prepare for your trip by figuring out all the specific details. Keep in mind that different locations and ways to travel require different skills and equipment. For example, an hour walk in the woods means you'd prepare by taking comfortable footwear, water, and an emergency kit. In contrast, an overnight canoe trip means preparing all that you'd need for the hike, plus a canoe, lifejackets, maps, tent, and so on. Preparing for your specific outing will ensure that you are safe, comfortable, and able to take full advantage of all that nature has to offer.

As you prepare, do a "reality check." Consider:

- Do you know enough about where you're going?
- Do you know enough about this type of outing?
- What skills and experience should someone have for this outing?
- Many outdoorsy types use the rule, "Hope for the best, but prepare for the worst." Have you prepared for the worst—a sudden storm? getting lost? bears?

When you've done your reality check, decide if you're ready or if you need to revise your plan and preparations. Hey, you can always take that more challenging trip another time, when you are truly ready for it.

PAY ATTENTION

So, you've planned, you've prepared, and now it's time to get active. To experience nature fully, use all of your senses during your outing. Watch the trail for wildlife, feel the wind on your face, listen to the birds, and smell the salt air. Paying close attention to your surroundings will not only deepen your enjoyment but also alert you to trouble. A careful eye, for example, will help prevent you from tripping over tree roots, alert you to a stormy sky, and help you stay with the group. Once you get out into Canada's great outdoors, keep safe and smiling by paying attention.

HELP!

How can you prepare for an emergency? Knowing how to use a first-aid kit, carrying an emergency whistle, and practising what to do if you get lost are all good general preparations. However, it is important to prepare for the hazards of each specific outing. For example, know about frostbite for winter hikes and safe swim rules for beach trips.

Reflect on

Strategies: Find three places in this article where using the unit strategies helped you understand what you were reading.

Connections: Think about books, TV shows, and news reports that show people in the great outdoors. What examples can you give of people who did not plan, prepare, and pay attention?

Credits

Text

10–16 © 1954 by James Ramsay Ullman. Reprinted by permission of HarperCollins Publishers and the Harold Matson Co., Inc. 20–26 From The Spirit of Canada: Canada's Story in Legends, Fiction, Poems and Song © 1999 Malcolm Lester Books. Reprinted by permission of Barbara Greenwood. 33–40 "Akla Gives Chase" from *Long Claws: An Arctic Adventure* by James Houston. Used by permission of McClelland & Stewart Ltd. 48–50 Text from *The Tree of Life* written by Rochelle Strauss, is used by permission of Kids Can Press Ltd., Toronto. Text © 2004 Rochelle Strauss. 54 Reprinted by permission of Canadian Geographic. 55 Courtesy of the Canadian Wildlife Federation, www.cwf-fcf.org. 56–58 Text from *Animals Eating* written by Pamela Hickman is used by permission of Kids Can Press Ltd., Toronto. Text © 2001 Pamela Hickman. 59–61 From *Coyotes in the Crosswalk: Canadian Wildlife in the City* by Diane Swanson © Diane Swanson 1994, Whitecap Books. 63–66 The Animal Notes: Polar Bear. From *Wild Science* by Victoria Miles © 2004 by Victoria Miles. Permission granted by Raincoast Books. 81 Used with permission of the publisher, Children's Book Press, San Francisco, CA, www.childrensbookpress.org. "Four Buffalo Spirits" from *This Land is My Land*, stories and pictures © 1993 by George Littlechild. 82–83 Used with permission of the publisher, Children's Book Press, San Francisco, CA, www.childrensbookpress.org. "I Love the Moon, the Stars, and the Ancestors" from *This Land is My Land*, stories and pictures © 1993 by George Littlechild. 84–86 From *Only In Canada!* By Vivien Bowers. Text © 2004 Vivien Bowers. Illustrations © 2004 Dianne Eastman. Reprinted by permission of Maple Tree Press. 87–89 Text and illustrations from The Kids Book of Canadian Exploration written by Ann-Maureen Owens and Jane Yealland. Illustrations by John Mantha. Used by permission of Kids Can Press Ltd., Toronto. Text © 2004 Ann-Maureen Owens and Jane Yealland. Illustrations © 2004 John Mantha. 90 Reprinted with permission of Key Porter Books. Copyright © 2000 by Janet Lunn and Christopher Moore. 92–95 Reprinted with permission of Key Porter Books. Copyright © 2000 by Janet Lunn and Christopher Moore. 96–100 Excerpted from The Museum Called Canada: 25 Rooms of Wonder by Charlotte Gray. Copyright artifact essays ©2004 Charlotte Gray. Copyright caption, text, design and compilation © 2004 Otherwise Inc. Reprinted by permission of Random House Canada. 104–106 Operation Brainwash from *Girl Zone Body Talk: The Straight Facts on Fitness, Nutrition & Feeling Great About Yourself.* By Ann Douglas and Julie Douglas, Maple Tree Press, Inc. 110–115 Reprinted by permission of KidsHealth. 116–118 Text and illustrations from Mysterious You: Burp! Written by Diane Swanson and illustrated by Rose Cowles, is used by permission of Kids Can Press Ltd., Toronto. Text © 2001 Diane Swanson. Illustrations © 2001 Rose Cowles. 119 © Made You Look: How Advertising Works and Why You Should Know by Shari Graydon. Published by Annick Press Ltd. 2003. Reprinted with permission. 120–121 Reading the Signals from Body Talk by Ann Douglas and Julie Douglas, Maple Tree Press. 122 Extracted from First Aid Training Brochure FA-500-E © 2007 The Priory of Canada of the Most Venerable Order of the Hospital of St. John of Jerusalem. 123 Reprinted by permission of Kids Help Phone.

Photos

Cover Clockwise © David A Northcott/Corbis, Digital Vision/Getty Images, McCord Museum 1775 M993.52.1 and 1840 M12678, © Tom Stewart Corbis. Unit Opener © Brad Wrobleski/ Masterfile. 18 Reprinted by permission of Penguin Group (USA) Inc. 19 Paramount/The Kobal Collection. 28 Getty Images. 30 AP/Laurence Kesterson. 31 Top to bottom AP/ Steve Helber, AP/Steve Helber. 32 Top to bottom Reuters/Landov, Reuters Landov. Unit Opener © Peter Johnson/Corbis. 42 Atlantic herring: Picture Press/Getty Images, garter snake: Shutterstock, vulture: Shutterstock, seal: Photos.com, catfish: Shutterstock, flamingo: Photos.com, pacific salmon: © Visual & Written SL/Alamy, bat: © Natural Visions/Alamy, hummingbird: Shutterstock, poison dart frog: Photos.com. 43 Chameleon: Photos.com, parrot: Shutterstock, turtle: Shutterstock, giant armadillo: Visual & Written SL/Alamy, cane toad: © Peter Arnold Inc/Alamy, lion: Photos.com, beluga whale: Shutterstock, crocodile: Shutterstock, peregrine falcon: Shutterstock, piranha: Shutterstock. 44 Jay Cossey/www.photographsfromnature.com. 45 Stone/GettyImages. 46 Clockwise from top right © Yann Arthus-Bertrand/Corbis, Shutterstock, Shutterstock, Photoresearchers/Firstlight.ca, Photoresearchers/Firstlight.ca. 47 Top to bottom Shutterstock, © Irwan/epa/Corbis, Shutterstock. 48–49 Shutterstock. 50 Shutterstock. 52–53 Ifremer/A.Fifis, Background © Robert George Young/Masterfile. 55 Cover photo and photos of butterfly, sea lion and Asian bull elephant courtesy of Wayne Lynch, ladybug photo courtesy of Robert McCaw, illustrations courtesy of Michel Poirier and Paul Robert. 56 Photos.com. 57 Dorling Kindersley/Getty Images. 58 Top to bottom Photoresearchers/Firstlight.ca, © Natural Visions/Alamy. 59 Creatas. 60 Victoria Hurst/Firstlight.ca. 61 Creatas/Firstlight.ca. 63 Top to bottom Raincoast Books, Dan Guravich/Corbis. 64–65 Shutterstock. 66 Norbert Rosing/National Geographic/Getty Images. Unit Opener J.D. Kelly/Rogers Communications. 68 Clockwise from top left Reprinted with permission of Gerald McMaster, Daphne Odjig, *Enfolding*, 1992 Serigraph on paper 53 x 42 cm, Kamloops Art Gallery Collection 1993-10, Kamloops Art Gallery Collecting Canadian Art Program. Photo by Vaughn Warren. Reprinted by permission of Stanley Somerville, © Ron Watts/Corbis. 69 Clockwise from top left *Flight* by Susan Point, Courtesy of Nance Ackerman, Courtesy of Alan Syliboy. 71 Top to bottom British Columbia Archives D-08249, Glenbow Archives NA-1727-67. 72 McCord Museum, M973.85.6A. 73 Top to bottom Courtesy of the artist Lewis Parker, Courtesy of Edmonton Tourism. 74 © Gunter Marx Photography/Corbis. 75 Top to bottom © Canadian Museum of Civilization, IV-D-505, image number S91-8364, Wave Eaters Exhibition, 1996 © CMC, photo Harry Foster, AC99-49.77 © Bridgeman Art Library/Superstock. 78 J.D. Kelly/Rogers Communications. 79 Library and Archives Canada, c-011226. 86 © Stuart Westmoreland/Corbis. 88 Top to bottom © D. Hurst/Alamy, Masterfile Royalty Free, Coronation Gulf, Hudson's Bay, Inuit traveling with dogs and sled with kayak on top, NWT © CMC, Stefansson Vilhjalmur, 19-?, 20288. 89 © Canadian Museum of Civilization, IV-D-505, image number S91-8364, Glenbow Archives, na-2360-1. 90 Carolyn A. McKeone/Photoresearchers/Firstlight.ca. 91 © Richard Emmons/Alamy. 92 Alan Daniel. 93 © doughoughton/Alamy. 94 © Greg Probst/Corbis. 95 Newfoundland Museum 4A600A1-76; 4A600A1-66a; 4A600A1-97 (replicas in exhibition). 96 Library and Archives Canada, c-041881. 98 Top to bottom Glenbow Archives NA-1532-4, The Manitoba Museum, HBC Archives. 99 Archives of Manitoba, Plate 59 (a) Indian Maps, 1801, Historical Atlas of Canada, University of Toronto Press. 100 Top to bottom Library and Archives Canada, c-02771, Bridgeman Art Library. Unit Opener Photos.com. 102 Clockwise from top left © Kevin Dodge/Corbis, vanhilversum/Alamy, David Young-Wolff/PhotoEdit Inc., © moodboard/Corbis, Michael Newman/PhotoEdit Inc., Gary Holscher/Getty Images, Jupiter Images/FoodPix/Firstlight.ca, © Jupiter Images/Thinkstock/Alamy. 104 © Ole Graf/Zefa/Corbis and Michael Newman/PhotoEdit Inc. 105 Clockwise from top © Jupiter Images/IT Stock Free/Alamy, © Design Pics Inc. Alamy, Miodrag Gajic/Shutterstock. 106 Top to bottom Filipchuk Oleg Vladimorich/Shutterstock, Tan Wei Ming/Shutterstock, © Blend Images/Alamy. 107 Photodisc/Getty Images, 108 © Colin Young-Wolff/Photoedit Inc. 116–118 Background image Shutterstock. 120 © Linda Matlow/Alamy. 125 Top to bottom © Tom Stewart/Corbis, © Blend Images/Alamy, 126 Top to bottom Shutterstock, © Image Source Pink/Alamy.

Art

8–9 illustrated by Paul Fricke. 10–16 illustrated by Carlos Martin Suaz. 17 illustrated by Brian McLachlan. 20–26 illustrated by Anton Petrov. 27 illustrated by James Yamasaki. 29 illustrated by Allan Moon. 56 illustrated by Brian McLachlan. 57 illustrated by Bart Vallecoccia. 62 illustrated by Jason Bone. 76 illustrated by Deborah Crowle. 80 illustrated by Deborah Crowle. 85 illustrated by Deborah Crowle. 87 illustrated by Greg Ruhl. 93 illustrated by Dave McKay. 97 illustrated by Dave McKay. 109 illustrated by Neil Babra. 110–115 illustrated by Ian Kim.